The Best of Grimm's Fairy Tales

Level 1
(1000-word)

Adapted by Ron Davidson

IBC パブリッシング

※本書はラダーシリーズ『グリム傑作童話集 (Grimms' Fairy Tales)』と
『グリム・クラシックス (Grimms' Classics)』を元に再構成したものです。

はじめに

　ラダーシリーズは、「はしご（ladder）」を使って一歩一歩上を目指すように、学習者の実力に合わせ、無理なくステップアップできるよう開発された英文リーダーのシリーズです。
　リーディング力をつけるためには、繰り返したくさん読むこと、いわゆる「多読」がもっとも効果的な学習法であると言われています。多読では、「1. 速く 2. 訳さず英語のまま 3. なるべく辞書を使わず」に読むことが大切です。スピードを計るなど、速く読むよう心がけましょう（たとえば TOEIC® テストの音声スピードはおよそ 1 分間に 150 語です）。そして 1 語ずつ訳すのではなく、英語を英語のまま理解するくせをつけるようにします。こうして読み続けるうちに語感がついてきて、だんだんと英語が理解できるようになるのです。まずは、ラダーシリーズの中からあなたのレベルに合った本を選び、少しずつ英文に慣れ親しんでください。たくさんの本を手にとるうちに、英文書がすらすら読めるようになってくるはずです。

《本シリーズの特徴》
- 中学校レベルから中級者レベルまで5段階に分かれています。自分に合ったレベルからスタートしてください。
- クラシックから現代文学、ノンフィクション、ビジネスと幅広いジャンルを扱っています。あなたの興味に合わせてタイトルを選べます。
- 巻末のワードリストで、いつでもどこでも単語の意味を確認できます。レベル1、2では、文中の全ての単語が、レベル3以上は中学校レベル外の単語が掲載されています。
- カバーにヘッドホーンマークのついているタイトルは、オーディオ・サポートがあります。ウェブから購入／ダウンロードし、リスニング教材としても併用できます。

《使用語彙について》

レベル1：中学校で学習する単語約1000語

レベル2：レベル1の単語＋使用頻度の高い単語約300語

レベル3：レベル1の単語＋使用頻度の高い単語約600語

レベル4：レベル1の単語＋使用頻度の高い単語約1000語

レベル5：語彙制限なし

Contents

Hansel and Gretel 1

The Frog Prince 25

The Bottled Spirit 35

The Shoes That Were Danced Full of Holes 49

The Three Spinning Women 61

The Fisherman and His Wife 69

The Brave Little Tailor 85

The Golden Goose 105

Word List 116

Hansel and Gretel

読みはじめる前に

Hansel and Gretel で使われている用語です。わからない語は巻末のワードリストで確認しましょう。

☐ branch	☐ gather	☐ tear
☐ cover	☐ grab	☐ thorn
☐ dawn	☐ hedge	☐ tie
☐ deer	☐ loosen	☐ wand
☐ feed	☐ palace	☐ wave
☐ flute	☐ stable	☐ yard
☐ force	☐ swan	
☐ form	☐ tap	

登場人物

Hansel ヘンゼル　貧しい木こりの息子。グレーテルの兄。

Gretel グレーテル　ヘンゼルの妹。

stepmother 継母　ヘンゼルとグレーテルの継母。2人を森に置き去りにする。

witch 魔法使いのおばあさん　お菓子の家の持ち主。

king 王様　森の中でヘンゼルとグレーテルに出会う。

用語解説

food shortage　食糧不足、飢饉。中世のヨーロッパでは深刻な不作や飢饉がたびたび起こった。

stepmother　継母。『白雪姫』や『シンデレラ』など、グリム童話には意地悪な継母がしばし登場する。
継父は「stepfather」。

Once upon a time, a poor woodcutter lived near a big woods with his wife and two children, a boy and a girl. The boy was called Hansel, and the girl, Gretel. They never had nice things to eat. Sometimes, when there was a food shortage in the land, they could not even get bread. One night, as the father lay in bed, he was very troubled.

"What will happen to us? How can we feed our little ones when we have nothing to eat ourselves?" he asked his wife.

"Listen," answered his wife, "early tomorrow morning we will take the children far into the woods, light them a fire, give each of them a piece of bread, then leave them alone. They will never find their way home and we will not have to feed them any more."

"No, wife," said the man, "I cannot do that. I cannot leave my two little children alone in the woods. They will probably be eaten by wild animals."

"Oh!" said she, "then all four of us will die of hunger." Finally, the poor woodcutter agreed to her plan.

The two children, however, were so hungry that they couldn't sleep. They had heard their stepmother's plan. Gretel said to Hansel, "We will die, dear brother."

"Don't cry Gretel," said Hansel, "I will make sure we don't die."

When the old folks went to sleep, Hansel put on his coat and quietly went out the back door. The moon was shining brightly and the white stones on the path in front of the house shone like silver coins. Hansel filled his pockets full of stones and returned to his room.

"Don't be afraid, little sister," he said to

Gretel, "God will not forget us. Now try to get some sleep."

Early the next day the woman called the two children.

"Get up, both of you," she said, "and come with us into the woods to gather sticks." She gave each of them a piece of bread and told them it was for dinner. She told them not to eat it because they would get nothing else.

Soon, they left together for the woods. They had not gone far when Hansel stopped. He looked back at the house. He did this again and again. His father said, "Hansel, what are you looking at?"

"Oh, father," said Hansel, "I am looking at my white dog sitting on the roof waving good-bye to me."

"That isn't your dog, you fool!" said his stepmother, "it's the morning sunlight shining on a stone." But Hansel had not really been looking at the dog; he was dropping the stones out of his pocket.

When they came to the middle of the woods the father said, "Now, children, gather sticks and we will make a fire."

Hansel and Gretel gathered up many sticks, and when the fire was burning strongly, the woman said, "You can lie down by the fire and rest yourselves while we go further to cut wood. When we have finished we will come and get you."

Hansel and Gretel sat by the fire. When dinner-time came, they ate their bread. They could still hear the sound of wood being cut. They thought that their father was close by. However, their father had tied a branch to a tree. Every time the wind blew, the branch hit the tree. This was the noise the children heard. They were very tired and soon they fell asleep in front of the fire. They did not wake up until it was night and very dark. Gretel began to cry, and said, "We shall never find our way out of the woods."

"Wait," said Hansel, "the moon will be up in a minute. Then we'll find our way out quickly."

Soon the great full moon rose in the sky, and Hansel took his little sister's hand and followed the stones. The stones shone brightly and showed them the way home. The children walked all night, and at dawn they reached their father's house. They knocked at the door and when the woman opened it and saw Hansel and Gretel she looked surprised. Then she quickly said, "Why did you sleep so long in the woods? We began to think you were not coming back at all."

The father was delighted to see the children. He felt that it was wrong to leave them alone and helpless.

A short time later, there was another food shortage.

The children heard their stepmother saying to their father, "There is hardly anything left to eat, only a little bread. What will we do when that is gone? We must leave the children in the forest. This time we will take them deeper into the woods, so that they will not be able to find their way out. It's the only thing we can do to save us."

The man's heart was heavy, and he thought, "I would rather share our last bread with the children." But the woman had made up her mind, and she would not listen to the man. He gave in the first time and he gave in the second time too.

The children, however, had heard everything. When his parents went to sleep, Hansel got up again to go out and pick up some stones. But, he couldn't go outside because the woman had closed the door. He said to his little sister, "Don't worry, Gretel, don't cry, go to sleep. God will take care of us."

The next morning the woman woke the children. She gave them each a piece of bread. It was a smaller piece of bread than last time.

As they walked to the woods Hansel broke the bread in his pocket and dropped little pieces on the ground.

The woman led the children deeper and deeper into the forest. She led them to a part they had never been before. Again, a large fire was made and their stepmother said, "Stay here, children, and when you are tired have a sleep. We are going further to cut wood. When we have finished we will come for you."

When dinner-time came Gretel shared her bread with Hansel, because he had dropped his as they walked along. Then they fell asleep. The evening went by and no one came to get them. When they awoke it was dark. Hansel said to his sister, "Wait till the moon is up, then we shall see the bread I dropped on the ground. The bread will show us the way home."

The moon rose, but they could see no bread. The birds in the woods had eaten every piece. The children still tried to find the way home. They walked the whole night and all the next day, but they were still in the woods. They were tired and hungry, and they lay down under a tree and fell asleep.

The next day they walked more. They both knew that they were deep in the woods. If help did not come soon they would die. Then they saw a beautiful snow-white bird sitting on a branch. It was singing so beautifully that they stopped to listen. When it finished its song, the bird flew in front of them. They followed it until it landed on the roof of a little house. It was a strange-looking house. When the children got closer they were happy to see that the house was built of bread. Its roof was made of cake and its windows were made of sugar.

"Okay," Hansel said, "let's have a good meal for a change. I will have a piece of the roof, and you have a nice, sweet window."

Hansel picked off a piece of the roof and began eating. Gretel stood by a window and ate some of it. Then a voice called from inside:

"Who's eating my house?"

The children answered:

"The wind, the wind, the child of heaven," and quietly continued eating.

Hansel thought the roof tasted very good. He tore off another big piece. Gretel took out the window and sat down to eat it. Suddenly the door opened and an old woman came out. Hansel and Gretel shook with fright. They dropped their food.

The old woman said, "Dear children, who brought you here? Come in and stay with me. You are safe with me!"

She took them by the hand and led them into the house. Inside, a good dinner was ready; milk, cakes, fruit and many other things the children had never even seen before. Afterwards, two little white beds were uncovered. Hansel and Gretel lay down in them and felt like they were in heaven.

The old woman, however, was not nice. She was really a witch. She caught the children who came to her house. After she caught them, she killed them. Then she cooked and ate them. The witch could not see far, but she had a good sense of smell. She could smell humans from far away. As soon as Hansel and Gretel came near her house, she had laughed, and said to herself, "I'll have them—they shall not escape."

Early the next morning, before the children were awake, the witch got up. When she saw their round, red faces, she thought, "What a tasty dish!" Then she grabbed Hansel and carried him to a little stable. She put him inside it and he could not escape. He shouted as loudly as he could, but it was no use. Next, the witch went to Gretel and cried, "Get up girl, and get some water to cook your brother something nice; he is outside in the stable and must be fattened up. When he is fat enough I shall eat him."

Gretel began to cry, but she was forced to do what the old witch told her to do.

From then on, Hansel was given lots of good food, but Gretel got only dry bread. Every morning the old witch went to the stable and said, "Hansel, put your finger out so that I can feel how fat you are getting." Hansel would put out a bone instead of a finger. The old woman, because she could not see well, wondered why Hansel did not grow fat.

After four weeks, Hansel was still thin. The witch decided she would wait no longer.

"Whether Hansel is fat or thin, I will kill and eat him tomorrow!"

The tears ran down the face of poor little Gretel.

"Dear God, help us!" she prayed. "If the

wild animals had eaten us in the woods we would at least have died together."

When the witch had gone, Gretel ran to Hansel and told him what the witch had said.

"We must escape somehow. If we don't she will kill us both."

Hansel said, "I know how to get out. I have loosened the window. But first you must get her magic wand so we can save ourselves if she follows us. Bring the flute that hangs in her room as well."

Gretel got both the wand and the flute, and the children escaped.

When the old witch came to see whether her dinner was ready, she saw they had escaped. She ran angrily to the window. Though her eyes were bad, she could see the children running away.

She quickly put on her magic shoes. The shoes could cover several yards with each step. She quickly caught up with the children. Gretel, however, had seen her coming. She used the magic wand and turned Hansel into a lake. She turned herself into a swan and stayed in the middle of the lake. The witch sat on the shore and tried to get the swan to come to her by throwing pieces of bread to it. Gretel did not go near, and at last the witch went home without the children.

Then Gretel used the wand to change herself and Hansel back, and they traveled on through the night. Gretel then turned herself into a beautiful rose in the middle of a thorny hedge, and Hansel sat by the side.

Soon the witch came along. She acted as if she did not know Hansel.

"Young man," she said, "may I pick that beautiful rose?"

"Oh yes," said Hansel.

She went to the hedge in a hurry to gather the flower, knowing that it was Gretel. Hansel pulled out his flute and began to play. The flute was a magic flute. Whoever heard the flute had to dance whether he wanted to dance or not. The old witch was forced to dance on and on. She could not stop to pick the rose. The thorns tore the clothes from her body and caught in her skin. Finally, she could not move.

Then Gretel used the magic wand to set herself free again and she and Hansel set out for home. After traveling a long way, Gretel grew tired. Both the children lay down to sleep. As they slept, the witch, who had escaped from the thorny hedge, came by. Seeing her magic wand, she picked it up and turned poor Hansel into a deer. She then decided to leave them in the woods to be eaten by wild animals. It was too much trouble to try and get them to her house again.

When Gretel woke and found what had happened she cried for poor Hansel. Beside her, tears rolled from Hansel's eyes, too.

Gretel said, "Rest, little deer; I will never leave you."

She took the poor deer with her as she tried to find her way home. At last they came to a little house. When Gretel found that no one lived there she decided she and Hansel would stay there.

She made a soft bed for the deer. Each morning she went out and gathered food for both of them. The deer ate out of her hand, and they played happily together. In the evening, when Gretel was tired, she laid her head on the deer and slept. If Hansel had had his own body they would have led a very happy life.

They lived like this for years and Gretel became a young woman. One day the king came to hunt there. When the deer heard the noise of the hunt, the dogs, the horses and the huntsmen, he wanted to see what was going on.

"Oh sister," he said, "let me go into the woods, so I can see what is happening."

He asked so often that at last Gretel let him go.

"But," she said, "be sure to come back in the evening. I shall close the door to keep out the huntsmen, but if you tap and say, 'Sister, let me in,' I shall know it is you. If you do not speak, I shall keep the door closed."

Hansel ran away as fast as he could, jumping high in the air in his happiness. The king and his huntsmen followed the beautiful animal, but could not catch him. Each time they thought they had him he would jump over a hedge and be out of sight again.

When it was dark Hansel ran home and said, "Sister, let me in!" Gretel opened the door and he jumped in. He was soon sleeping soundly on his soft bed.

Next morning the hunt continued and when he heard the noise, the deer said, "Sister, open the door. I must go."

Once again the king and huntsmen followed the little deer. The hunt lasted all day. Near evening one of the hunters hit the deer in the foot. Although he was hurt, Hansel got home before he was caught. The hunter followed Hansel and heard the little deer say, "Sister, let me in." The man saw the deer go inside the house. The huntsman ran to the king and told him what he had seen.

"Tomorrow," said the king, "we shall have another hunt and this time we shall catch this deer."

Gretel was very upset when she saw that

Hansel was hurt. She washed the blood away and put some magic on his foot. Then they went to sleep.

In the morning there was no mark anywhere on the deer's foot. When Hansel heard the hunt starting again he said, "I must go Gretel, but I will take care they don't catch me."

But Gretel was still upset from the night before.

"I am sure they will kill you this time: I will not let you go."

"I shall die," said Hansel, "if you keep me here." Gretel was not happy but she had to let him go, and he quickly ran off into the woods.

When the king saw the deer he said to his men, "Follow him all day long until you catch him, but do not hurt him." The deer was too fast for them, however. When evening came, the king told his men to stop.

"Show me where the little house is," he said to the man who had followed the deer the day before. When they got to the house the king knocked on the door and said "Sister, let me in."

The door opened and the king went in. He saw the most beautiful girl he had ever seen.

Gretel was very frightened when she saw that it was not the deer but a king who had entered her house, but the king spoke kindly. After a while he took her hand and said, "Will you come to my palace and be my wife?"

"Yes," replied Gretel, "I will come to your palace but I cannot be your wife, and my deer must go with me for I cannot part with him."

"Well," said the king, "he shall come and live with you all your life. He will have everything he wants."

Just then the little deer came home. Soon, everyone was ready to leave. The king lifted Gretel onto his horse and they rode to his palace. The deer ran happily behind them. On the way Gretel told the king her story. He knew the old witch and her bad ways and sent for her the next day. He ordered her to change the deer back into human form.

When she saw her dear brother again Gretel was very thankful. She agreed to marry the king. They lived happily for the rest of their lives. Hansel became the king's right-hand man.

The Frog Prince

読みはじめる前に

The Frog Prince で使われている用語です。わからない語は巻末のワードリストで確認しましょう。

- ☐ carriage
- ☐ crown
- ☐ faithful
- ☐ ignore
- ☐ iron
- ☐ plate
- ☐ shade
- ☐ stick
- ☐ upset
- ☐ waterhole
- ☐ well

登場人物

princess お姫様　王様の末娘。

frog かえる　魔法によってかえるに変身させられた王子。

Henry ヘンリー　王子の忠臣。

In the good old days, when wishes often came true, there lived a king. All his daughters were beautiful. The youngest princess was so beautiful that even the sun was surprised every time it kissed her face.

Close to the king's home was a dark forest. In the forest under an old tree was a waterhole. The princess often went to the waterhole on hot days. She sat on the bank by the cool water. She loved playing with a special golden ball. She would throw the ball high in the air and then catch it.

One day, instead of falling into her little hands, the princess' golden ball rolled along the ground into the water. The princess went to the well to look for her ball. The well was so deep, however, that she could not see the bottom. She began to cry. She cried louder and louder. Then a voice called out, "Why, princess, what is the matter? You cry so loudly even a stone would feel sorry for you." She looked round to see who was talking and saw a frog with its head sticking out of the water.

The frog was not very pretty, but the princess told him about her problem.

"Well, stop your crying right now," said the frog, "I can help you. What will you give me if I get your ball for you?"

"Anything you like, my dear frog," she said: "I would give you my clothes, my riches, or even my crown."

The frog thought about this for a moment and then said, "Thank you princess, but I don't want any of these things. What I want is your love. I want to be your friend. I want you to play with me and to let me sit next to you at your table. Let me eat off your plate and share your little bed with you. If you do, I will get your golden ball from the bottom of the well."

"Okay," she said. "I'll promise anything you like if you get my ball back for me." The frog disappeared into the well and the princess thought, "What a fool the frog is! He can only sit in the water and talk to other frogs, he can't be friends with humans."

In a little while the frog came back with the ball in his mouth. He threw it to the princess. She was so happy to get it back. She picked it up and ran away.

"Stop! Stop! Take me with you, I can't run so fast," shouted the little frog. It was no use. Even though he shouted as loudly as he could the princess ignored him. Soon she got home and she quickly forgot all about the little frog who had helped her. The frog sadly went back into his well.

The next day the princess sat down to eat with the king and the rest of her family. She was eating off her little gold dish when she heard a strange noise. Something jumped up the stairs, knocked on the door and said, "Young princess, let me in!" She ran to the door and saw the frog. She shut the door quickly and went back to her seat. She was very afraid.

The king saw this and said, "Child, why are you afraid? What is at the door?"

"A frog," she answered.

"What does the frog want with you?" asked the king.

"Well, dear father, yesterday, when I was playing in the forest, my golden ball fell into the well. I started crying and the frog heard me. He got the ball back for me. I promised him he could be my friend, but I never thought he would come so far out of his water. Now he is outside and wants to come in." There was another knock at the door and the frog called:

"Open the door, my princess, dear,
Open the door to your true love here!
Remember the promise you yesterday made
By the cool well, in the old tree's shade."

Then the king said, "You must not break your promise. Go and let him in."

She went and opened the door, and the frog jumped in. He followed her to her chair and said, "Lift me up."

She did not want to lift him up, but the king ordered her to do so. The frog got onto the table and said, "Push your little gold dish near me so that we can eat together." The princess pushed her plate near the frog but she was not happy. The frog ate a lot, but the princess ate nothing. At last the frog said, "I am full. Now I am tired. Take me to your little room, put me in your bed and we will lie down and go to sleep."

The princess began to cry. She could not bring herself even to touch the cold frog. She did not want him sleeping in her pretty, clean bed.

The king became angry with her and said, "We must not forget the people who have helped us."

So, the princess lifted up the frog, carried him upstairs and put him in a corner of her room. When she was in bed the frog came over to her and said, "I am tired, I

THE FROG PRINCE

would like to go to bed too. Lift me up, please, or I'll tell your father." Then the princess got really angry. She picked the frog up and threw him against the wall.

"You bad frog," she shouted.

When he fell to the ground, however, he was no longer a frog. He was a prince, with beautiful, smiling eyes. He told the princess how an old witch had changed him into a frog. Nobody except the young princess had the power to change him back.

"Tomorrow we will travel back to my kingdom together," he said. They slept happily, and when the sun came up the next morning, a carriage with eight white horses arrived at the door. Behind the horses stood Henry, the faithful servant of the young prince. Henry was so upset when his master was turned into a frog. Henry had put three rings of iron around his heart to stop it breaking from sadness.

The carriage set off for the prince's land with the prince and the princess happy together inside the carriage and Henry outside, driving. They had not gone far when the young couple heard a noise as if something was breaking. They heard the same noise three times. They thought something in the carriage had broken. However, when they looked outside they saw that it was only the iron rings breaking from Henry's heart, because he was so happy.

The Bottled Spirit

読みはじめる前に

The Bottled Spirit で使われている用語です。わからない語は巻末のワードリストで確認しましょう。

- ☐ branch
- ☐ complete
- ☐ fearlessly
- ☐ fool
- ☐ force
- ☐ heal
- ☐ hurt
- ☐ measure
- ☐ neighbor
- ☐ offer
- ☐ please
- ☐ praise
- ☐ run
- ☐ soil
- ☐ worth

登場人物

woodcutter 木こり 貧しいながらも息子を学校に通わせていた。

son 木こりの息子 優秀な学生だったが、修了前に学費が底をつく。

spirit おばけ 小さな瓶の中に閉じ込められているが、瓶から出ると巨大化する。

There was once a poor woodcutter who worked every day from early in the morning till late at night. After a long time he had saved a little money and he said to his son, "You are my only child, so I will give you the money I have made from my hard work. Spend it on your schooling. Learn something useful so you will be able to look after me when I am old."

The boy went to school and studied very hard. His teachers praised him for his work. After a few years he was able to go to college. Before he could complete his studies, however, he ran out of money and was forced to leave school. He returned to his father, who was very unhappy. "I have no more money," said the old woodcutter, "and the pay I get for woodcutting is only enough to buy food to eat."

"Don't worry father," answered the son, "If this is what God wants, it must be good."

The next day, the old man was getting ready to go to work. His son offered to go with him.

"Yes, my son, come; but it will be difficult for you. You are not used to such hard work. Also, I only have one ax."

"Never mind," said the son, "we will borrow an ax from our neighbor until I can buy a new one."

The neighbor kindly agreed and they set off together for the forest. All morning they worked and the son was pleased to be helping his father. The father was glad to have his son with him.

When the sun was at its highest the old man said, "We will rest now and have our lunch."

The son ate his bread but then instead

of resting like his father, he walked in the forest. Everything was new and interesting to him.

"Where are you going, my son? You should rest and not tire yourself out."

"I won't go far, father. It's just that it feels good to be in the forest among the birds and trees."

He walked some more and came to a big old tree. He walked around the tree to get an idea of its size.

"Well, old tree, many birds have made their homes in your branches," he said quietly, as he looked up at the tree.

Then he thought he heard a voice. He listened very hard. He could just hear a voice saying, "Let me out! Let me out!"

He looked around but could see nothing so he called out. "Where are you? I can't see you."

"I'm over here," the voice answered, "in

the ground under the big tree."

The student looked under the tree and started to move the soil away. Before long he found a bottle. When he held it up to the light he saw there was something inside the bottle. It was jumping up and down like a frog.

"Let me out! Let me out!" it cried again. The student felt sorry for it. He took out the stopper. As soon as he did so a spirit came out of the bottle. It grew and grew until it was almost half the size of the tree. It looked down at the student below it.

"Do you know," asked the spirit in a deep, low voice, "what you will get for letting me out of the bottle?"

"No," replied the student fearlessly, "How could I know?"

"I must break your neck!" answered the spirit.

"I'm sorry that you didn't tell me that

The Bottled Spirit

before I let you out. But you will have to wait. There are other people we must talk to before you can break my neck."

"People or no people, I must break your neck. When I was put in the bottle I had to promise that if I ever escaped I would break the neck of whoever let me out."

"Oh well," replied the student coolly, "if you must, you must. But first you must prove to me, that it was really you who sat in the bottle. If you can get in the bottle again I will be sure it was you. Then you can do what you like with me."

The spirit said it was very easy to get back into the bottle. He got smaller and smaller until he was able to get back into the bottle. As soon as the spirit was in the bottle the student pushed the stopper back in.

As soon as he realized what had happened the spirit began to shout, "Let me out! Oh please, let me out!" The student put the bottle on the forest floor and began to walk away.

"Come back, please! If you let me out I will give you something that will make you rich for the rest of your life."

"How do I know that you are not trying

to fool me?" replied the student.

"I promise I will not hurt you in any way if you let me out. If you don't let me out you will miss a chance to be happy forever."

The student thought a long time and then decided to take the chance. He removed the stopper and once again the spirit grew bigger and bigger until the student could hardly see the sky.

"Now I will do as I promised," said the spirit. He gave the student a magic wand and said, "If someone is in pain, and you touch the place it hurts with one end of this wand, they will get better. If you touch something made of iron with the other end of the wand, the iron will be turned into silver."

"Here, let me try it," said the student. He took the wand and went over to a tree that had a piece cut out of it and touched it. Straight away the cut was replaced and the tree looked healthy and strong. "It really is a magic wand. You have done as you promised."

The student and the spirit thanked each other and said good-bye.

When the student returned to his father, the old man asked him where he had been for such a long time. "I knew you would never make it as a woodcutter," he said sadly.

"Don't be upset father; I will soon make everything right."

The son picked up his ax and touched it with the wand. "I'll cut down this tree with one blow," he said and gave the tree a mighty hit. However, because the ax was now made of silver it nearly broke.

"What have you done?" shouted the father. "We cannot return this ax to our neighbor. We'll have to buy a new one. But, what can we buy a new ax with? We have no money."

"Father, it's not so bad," said the son, "I can pay for the ax."

"You fool! How can you pay for the ax? You have no money. I should never have let you come woodcutting."

The son waited a while then said, "Father, I can't work any more today. Let's take the rest of the day off."

"You aren't thinking straight, you young fool. Even if you don't want to work, I must work. If I don't work, we will have nothing to eat tonight. You go home. You are no use in the forest anyway."

"I can't find my way home alone. It's my first time in the forest. Come with me please."

The father became less angry and after a few more words he took his son home. When they were near their house the father sent his son to the market to try and sell the broken ax. "Get a good price, for I will have to save money to buy a new one."

The son went to the silver shop in town. When the owner of the shop measured the weight of the ax he said, "This is worth four hundred dollars. But now, I only have three hundred dollars. I will pay you the other hundred when I get it next month."

The son was very happy. When he

arrived home he said, "Father, I have some money. Tell me how much a new ax costs."

"One dollar," replied the father.

"Well, give our neighbor two dollars, I'm sure he'll be happy with that. I have a lot of money. Here, take this," said the son, handing over one hundred dollars. "You shall always have everything you want."

"Goodness me," cried the old man, "where did all this money come from?"

The father could hardly believe it when the student told him the story of the bottled spirit.

After a while, the father got used to not working anymore. The son used the rest of the money to finish college. Once again, his teachers were pleased with his work. In time, because his wand could heal all illnesses, the student became the most famous doctor in the world.

The Shoes That Were Danced Full of Holes

読みはじめる前に

The Shoes That Were Danced Full of Holes で使われている用語です。わからない語は巻末のワードリストで確認しましょう。

- [ ] announcement
- [ ] barely
- [ ] branch
- [ ] lord
- [ ] pretend
- [ ] prove
- [ ] row
- [ ] shore
- [ ] snore

登場人物

twelve princesses 12人のお姫様　同じ部屋で一列に並んで眠る。戸締りをしているのに、朝になると靴がすりきれている。

poor soldier 貧しい兵士　すりきれた靴の謎に挑む。

old woman 老婆　貧しい兵士に不思議な古いコートを授ける。

Once upon a time there was a king who had twelve beautiful daughters. They slept together in a long room and their beds stood close together in a row. Each night the king would shut the bedroom door so that no one could get in or out.

In the morning, however, when he opened the door, it was always the same. The girls' shoes had been danced full of holes. No one knew how this could happen. The girls always said that they had slept soundly through the night.

The king could not find out what happened. He decided to find someone who could find out what happened. The king made an announcement to everyone in the country. Whoever could find out how the shoes were danced full of holes could marry one of his daughters. The man could be the next king. However, anyone who tried but was not successful in three days, would have his head cut off.

Soon a young prince became the first to try and find the answer. The king was very nice to him and made him feel most welcome. A bed was put in the hall near the princesses' room for him. At night, the prince lay outside waiting to see what happened.

After a little while, however, his eyes began to feel very heavy and soon he was asleep. When he awoke in the morning it was clear that the twelve sisters had been to a dance. There were holes in all their shoes. The second and third night the prince failed again. On the fourth morning, his head was cut off.

Other princes and lords came and tried to find the answer. All of them fell asleep and all of them lost their heads.

One day, a poor soldier came to the city. When an old woman asked him why he had come, he laughed and said, "Maybe, I will try and find out what happens at night in the princesses' bedroom. If I succeed I will be the next king. Not a bad price for three nights' work."

Although he probably had not meant what he said the old woman believed him. She quickly said, "It is not so difficult. Do not drink the wine they bring you at night. Pretend to drink it and pretend to fall asleep." Then she gave the poor soldier an old coat. "If you throw this over yourself no one will be able to see you. Then you can follow the twelve girls and see where they go."

The soldier went to the king and offered to find the answer to the problem. Even though he was not a lord or prince, the king was kind to him and wished him good luck.

At bedtime, the soldier was led to the hall outside the girls' room. When he was getting into bed, the oldest princess brought him a glass of wine. When she was not looking, he quickly poured the wine on the ground behind. Then he held the glass to his mouth like he had drunk it. He then lay down and after a few minutes began to breathe heavily as if he were sleeping.

The twelve princesses heard his snores

and the oldest said, "He, too, could have saved himself trouble, and his life!"

Then the princesses got up and put on their best clothes. They laughed and sang and thought about the dancing they were going to do.

The youngest princess seemed a little unhappy and said, "I don't feel good about this evening. Something will go wrong, I can feel it."

"Don't be a fool," said the oldest princess, "what is there to be afraid of? Remember all the princes who tried to find out what we do at night. How could this poor soldier do any better? I gave him the wine. He won't wake up before morning."

Before they left, the princesses looked at the soldier again. He seemed to be asleep. The oldest daughter went to the head of her bed and hit it. The floor opened up in a secret opening and the girls went down through the opening. The soldier, who had been watching them, put on his magic coat and followed close behind the youngest princess. He got too close, however, and stepped on her dress. She shouted, "Who is that? Someone stepped on my dress."

"There's no one there," said the oldest, "you must have caught it on something." The princesses continued down the stairs to the bottom. In front of them was a small forest of beautiful trees. A winding road went through the forest. The girls went into the forest. The soldier thought he might have to prove what had happened so he broke a branch off a tree. The youngest princess heard it and said, "What was that? Didn't you hear a noise?"

"It was one of our princes firing a gun to welcome us," said the oldest princess.

The princesses continued down the road and soon came to a lake. There were twelve boats on the shore. Next to each boat stood a tall prince. The princes and princesses paired off and each pair got into a boat. The soldier quickly got into the boat with the youngest princess. After a while her prince said, "Why does the boat seem so much heavier than usual? I can barely move it tonight."

"It must be the weather," replied the youngest princess, "it's so hot I can hardly breathe."

On the other side of the lake was a beautiful palace. There were bright lights everywhere and the sound of music could be heard across the water. The boats landed and the princes and the princesses entered the palace. They started dancing and the soldier watched them. The youngest princess stopped to drink some wine, but the soldier drank it from her glass before she could drink it.

The youngest princess was surprised and afraid. Again her older sisters told her everything was okay. They danced until three o'clock in the morning. By then their shoes were full of holes and they could dance no more.

As they were going home the soldier quietly moved ahead of them and arrived home before them. When the princesses got home he was back in bed and he looked like he had never moved.

The next morning, the soldier said nothing. He watched the same thing happen on the second and third nights. To help prove his story he took a glass from the palace and some water from the lake.

On the fourth morning, he put the branch, and the glass and water under his coat and went to the king.

The king asked, "Where do my daughters dance their shoes full of holes each night?"

The soldier said:

"In an underground palace, across a lake, with twelve princes." He showed the king the branch, glass, and water and told him the full story

The king called for his daughters. He asked them if the soldier was telling the truth. The girls saw the glass and the branch from the beautiful forest and they knew the soldier knew their secret.

Then the king said "Which of my

daughters do you want to marry?"

"I am not so very young," said the soldier, "I will marry the oldest one."

They married and soon after the soldier became the next king.

The Three Spinning Women

読みはじめる前に

The Three Spinning Women で使われている用語です。わからない語は巻末のワードリストで確認しましょう。

- [ ] empty
- [ ] material
- [ ] moment
- [ ] please
- [ ] spin
- [ ] spinning wheel
- [ ] suppose
- [ ] thread
- [ ] upset
- [ ] wet
- [ ] yell

登場人物

girl 女の子　怠け者で母親に叱られている。

queen 女王　糸を紡ぐよう、女の子を城に連れてくる。

old women 老女たち　1人は右足が、1人は口が、もう1人は片方の腕が異様に大きい。

Once upon a time, there was a girl who would not work. She was supposed to work at the spinning wheel making thread. One day her mother got very angry and began hitting her. "Oh, why won't you work like other girls?" the mother yelled.

The queen, who happened to be passing, heard the yelling and she went into the house. She asked the mother why she was hitting her daughter. The woman did not want to say it was because her daughter would not work, so she said, "I cannot get her away from the spinning wheel, and I am poor and cannot buy the material she needs to make thread."

The queen said, "Perhaps I can help you, I have a lot of material at the palace. I would love it if your daughter came along and worked for me."

Of course the mother agreed to this. When they arrived at the palace the queen showed the daughter three rooms. They were all large rooms, and they were all full of material waiting to be turned into thread.

"Here you are, my dear, if you spin all this into thread you can marry my oldest son."

The girl was left alone and quickly started to cry. She knew that even if she worked for a hundred years she would not finish the job the queen had given her.

For three days she cried and she wondered what the queen would say when she found out that she was not working. She went to the window and thought sadly of her family. Looking down, she saw three old women outside the palace. One had a large right foot, one had a mouth twice the usual size, and the third had one arm bigger than any man's.

The old women saw that the girl was upset and asked her what the problem was. She told them and they said, "If you ask us to your wedding and tell everybody we are your aunts, we will do all the work for you."

"I will, of course I will," said the young girl happily.

She let in the three strange-looking old women and they began to spin. The girl did not let the queen know about the three women, and the queen was very pleased at the amount of thread being made.

Soon all the material had been spun into thread. As the three strange women left the palace, one of them said to the girl "Remember your promise to us. Ask us to come when you get married and you will have great happiness."

When the girl showed the queen the empty rooms the queen was so happy that she set the date for the marriage right away.

The girl said, "I would like my three aunts to come on the marriage day. They are three old women but they have been very kind to me. If you will allow it I would like them to share our table."

The queen and the prince agreed. When the day came, the spinning women arrived and they looked very strange. The girl quickly welcomed them and said, "Come and sit at my table, my dear aunts, next to the prince and I."

When he saw them the prince was quite upset. "Why," he asked his wife, "are your aunts so strange-looking?" Then he turned to one and asked, "How come you have such a large foot?"

"From spinning the wheel," she said.

"And how come you have such a big mouth?" he said to the next.

"From wetting the material," the second woman said.

"And you," he said to the third. "Why is your right arm so big, when your left one is the usual size?"

"From holding the thread," she said.

"Well then," said the prince after thinking for a moment. "My beautiful wife will never touch a spinning wheel again, even though she is so good at it!"

The Fisherman and His Wife

読みはじめる前に

The Fisherman and His Wife で使われている用語です。わからない語は巻末のワードリストで確認しましょう。

- ☐ contain
- ☐ countryside
- ☐ guard
- ☐ lord
- ☐ master
- ☐ ladies-in-waiting
- ☐ mighty
- ☐ nevertheless
- ☐ remain
- ☐ reply
- ☐ ruler
- ☐ shore
- ☐ stand
- ☐ suppose
- ☐ throne
- ☐ unpleasant
- ☐ upset

登場人物

fisherman 漁師　海のそばの古い家で、おかみさんと暮らしている。心優しいが気が弱く、おかみさんに逆らえない。

fisherman's wife 漁師のおかみさん　ごうつくばりで、不思議な魚にいろいろなものを要求する。

fish 魚　魔法が使える不思議な魚。逃がしてくれたお礼に、漁師のおかみさんの願いを次々にかなえてあげる。

There was once a fisherman who lived with his wife close to the sea. Their house was very old, and the rooms were small and dark. The woman found it very unpleasant to live there and wanted to move somewhere nicer, but they did not have the money.

One day, when he was fishing, the fisherman pulled in his line and on the end was the biggest fish he had ever caught.

To his surprise the fish started talking, "Listen fisherman," he said, "please don't kill me for I am not really a fish, I am a magic prince. You would not enjoy it if you ate me, so put me back in the water."

"Well," said the fisherman, "I wouldn't think of keeping a fish that could speak." He quickly put the fish back in the water and watched as it swam away in the clear, blue sea. He caught nothing else that day and went home to his wife in their old house.

"Have you not caught anything today, husband?"

"No," replied he, "I did catch one fish, a great big one, in fact, but he said he was a magic prince, so I let him go."

"You let him go, did you? I suppose you didn't ask for anything, did you?"

"No, I didn't. What should I have wished for?"

"You know I can't stand this old house, you should have asked him for a nice new one. Go back to the sea and call to him and tell him we want a new house. I'm sure he'll give us one."

The man did not really want to go, but he did not want to upset his wife either, so off he went to the sea.

When he reached the sea, he noticed that the waves were a little higher and the sea a darker blue. He went to the shore and said:

"Great fish in the sea, please listen to me,
My wife won't let be, as I'd have it be."

When he had finished, the fish he had caught earlier came swimming up and said, "What does she want?"

"Well," said the man, "my wife thinks that because I let you go, I should have wished for something. I should have asked you for a new house as she does not like our old one."

"Go home," said the fish, "she has one already."

The man went home and found that in place of his old home was a new house. Indeed, everything in it was new: the kitchen, the bed, and they even had a little garden with all kinds of fruit trees. "This is much better," said his wife.

"Yes, we'll stay here and be very happy," replied the man.

"We'll see about that," said his wife quietly.

Everything was fine for the next two weeks but then the wife said, "Listen, husband, this new house is too small, far too small, and I need a bigger garden as well. Go back to the fish and tell him we want something bigger, like a nice, stone palace."

"No, wife," replied the fisherman, "the

fish has already given us this house. I don't want to go to him again; he might be angry with me."

"Just go, will you? He will be happy to do it for the man who saved his life."

The man's heart was heavy, and he objected to going. He thought to himself that it wasn't right, but before long he found himself at the seashore looking at a sea that seemed almost angry. Nevertheless he called out to the fish:

"Great fish in the sea, please listen to me,
My wife won't let be, as I'd have it be."

"Well, what does she want this time?" said the fish. "Oh," said the man a little fearfully, "she wants to live in a stone palace."

"Go home," said the fish, "she is standing in front of the door right now."

When the man arrived at the place where his house had been he found a great stone palace, and his smiling wife waiting on the steps.

"Well, aren't you coming in then," she said taking his arm. They entered the palace together. Their mouths dropped open in surprise. Everything was so beautiful. The walls were shiny and new, and there were beautiful, brightly colored things in every room. Behind the house was a large yard containing horses, dogs and many other farm animals; beyond the house was a great garden more than two miles long, filled with flowers, plants and beautiful trees.

"Well," said the wife, "Isn't this fine?"

"Yes," said the man, "and it shall remain so. We'll stay in this beautiful palace and be happy forever."

"We'll see about that," replied his wife quietly.

The next morning the wife woke first. The sun had just risen and she could see the beautiful countryside out of her bedroom window. When she heard her husband waking up, she pushed him out of bed saying, "Come over here to the window. Look at this beautiful land. Why can't we be rulers of it? Go to the fish and tell him we want to be rulers of this land."

"Oh, wife!" said the man, "why should we be rulers? I don't want to be a ruler."

"Well, I do," shouted his wife, "now get to the fish and tell him to make us rulers."

The man went to the seashore. For the first time in his life he was afraid of the sea, for the waves were high and came rushing up the shore. Nevertheless he stood by the ocean and said:

"Great fish in the sea, please listen to me,
My wife won't let be, as I'd have it be."

"What does she want this time?" said the fish.

"Oh," said the man, almost as though he was talking to himself, "she wants to be ruler of our land."

"Go home," said the fish, "she has her wish."

The man went home, and as he got nearer to the stone palace he saw that it had got much larger. There were soldiers standing guard outside and servants running here and there. Inside, there were beautiful paintings on the walls, and almost everything seemed to be made of gold. The doors of the main hall opened into the biggest room he had ever seen.

In the middle of the room, with six ladies-in-waiting on either side of her, was his wife. She was seated high on a throne with a gold crown on her head. The fisherman went up to her and said "Well wife, you are ruler now."

"Yes," she replied, "I am."

He stood for a while looking at her and then said, "How great it is that you are ruler; now we won't wish for anything more."

"Not at all, husband," answered the wife and she became quite angry, "I'm getting tired of all this, and I can't stand it any longer. I must be queen of this country."

"Oh no, wife, not that. Why do you want to be queen, isn't this enough?"

His wife looked at him with her face set hard, "I want to be queen and I will be queen."

"But wife," cried the fisherman, "the fish, even though he is magic, cannot make you queen. There is only one queen in the country; the fish can't make you queen, I'm sure he can't."

"Don't say 'can't' to me, for I am a ruler,

and you're only my husband. Now be off to the fish and get him to make me queen."

The man went off to the shore. He was unhappy and knew there was something wrong when he saw the sea. It was black and angry-looking and a great wind was driving the waves onto the shore. He stood by the edge and said:

"Great fish in the sea, please listen to me,
My wife won't let be, as I'd have it be."

"What does she want?" asked the fish.

"I am unhappy to say that she wants to be queen."

"Go home," said the fish, "she is queen already."

So the man went home and when he returned it looked as if the whole palace was made of gold. There were a great many soldiers, and hundreds of lords and ladies waiting in a beautiful room, which stretched as far as the eye could see. In the middle of the room, on a stand hundreds of feet high was a golden throne on which his wife sat.

When the man at last got close to her, he said, "Wife, are you queen now?"

"Yes," she replied, "I'm queen."

The man looked at her for a while and

then he said, "How great it is that you are queen. It's hard to believe. You cannot possibly want anything else."

His wife just looked at him for a while but said nothing. The fisherman went to bed that night with an uneasy feeling. When he did fall asleep, he slept very soundly, for he had walked a long way that day. His wife, the new queen, however, could not get to sleep. She turned from side to side all night wondering what else she could ask for. At the break of day she saw the sun come up. "Ha!" she thought, "could I not order the sun and the moon to appear when I want them to?"

"Husband," she said, and hit him in the side with her arm, "wake up; go to the fish and tell him I want to control the sun and moon."

The man was still half asleep but he was so afraid that he fell out of bed. "What did you say, wife?"

"Husband, if I can't order the sun and moon to come up then I don't see the point in having everything else. Go now, to the fish, I want to be master of the sun and moon."

"Oh no!" said the man falling to his knees, "the fish can't do that. He has made you queen, be happy with that."

His wife looked at him and became almost mad with anger. She tore at her clothes then gave her husband a mighty push, "Go to the fish this minute. I can't stand this any longer." The man ran off afraid of going to the sea, but more afraid of his wife. Outside there was a storm, the like of which the man had never seen before. The wind blew cold rain into his face as he stood facing the sea. The waves were as high as mountains and the water looked black with anger. In his fear he cried out:

"Great fish in the sea, please listen to me,
My wife won't let be, as I'd have it be."

"What does she want?" asked the fish.

"My wife wants to be master of the sun and moon."

"Go home," said the fish, "she is back in your old house already."

And there they have remained to this day.

The Brave Little Tailor

読みはじめる前に

The Brave Little Tailor で使われている用語です。わからない語は巻末のワードリストで確認しましょう。

- [ ] branch
- [ ] companion
- [ ] doubtful
- [ ] fellow
- [ ] fly
- [ ] fulfill
- [ ] hedge
- [ ] honor
- [ ] madman
- [ ] nail
- [ ] promise
- [ ] resign
- [ ] save
- [ ] sticky
- [ ] strength
- [ ] stroke
- [ ] trunk

登場人物

tailor 仕立て屋 主人公の小柄な仕立て屋。甘いものが好き。

giant 巨人 山に住む大男。仕立て屋と力比べをする。

king 王様 仕立て屋をとても強い男だと信じ込み、兵士として召し抱える。

One fine summer morning, a little tailor sat at his table by the window working as fast as he could. As he was working, a country woman came down the road outside his house calling, "Lovely sweets, get your lovely sweets here." The little tailor loved sweets so he called out of the window, "Come up here my dear woman, for here is a market for your goods."

The woman climbed the stairs with her heavy bag and unpacked all her sweets. After smelling all of them the tailor chose one. It was a sticky, sugary sweet that he was sure he would enjoy. "I'll take half a small bag of this one," he said, at last. The woman, who had hoped to sell a lot more than that, gave him the small bag and went on her way looking rather unkindly at the tailor. "I shall not eat these sweets right away," cried the tailor, "No, I will save them until I have finished work." So he laid the sweets on a table by the wall and went back to the clothes he was making.

The smell of the sweets, however, caused many flies to come to the tailor's room. They landed on the sweets and began tasting them.

"Who said you could have some?" said the little tailor as he attempted to drive them away. But the flies did not understand his language and they came back for more in greater numbers. Then the little tailor became really angry and hit at the flies with a cloth. He got seven, all dead with their legs in the air, at one stroke.

"What a man I am," he said, "the whole town should hear of what I have done." As fast as he could, he cut himself a belt, and on it he wrote the words, "Seven at one stroke!" Proudly, he put it on and looked at himself.

"No, not the whole town, but the whole world should know of me." The tailor looked around his room realizing that it had become too small for someone as mighty as he. He decided to leave. The only thing he took with him was a small piece of cheese, which he put in his pocket.

He decided to journey throughout the world until he was famous everywhere. As he rushed outside he saw a bird caught in a hedge. Feeling sorry for it he gently picked it out and put it in his pocket with the cheese.

He stepped out happily, and being small and light he could walk a long way without feeling tired. The road led to a mountain, but the tailor just kept going up and up. When he reached the highest point he found a powerful giant sitting there. The tailor was not afraid and he went up to the giant and said, "Good day, friend. Are you sitting here looking at the great world beyond? I am on my way there, do you want to come with me?"

The giant looked down upon the tailor, "You," he said in a deep, loud voice, "who are you to offer yourself as a traveling companion for a giant? You are a weak nobody."

"You think so, do you?" replied the tailor, "well, just you look at this." He opened his coat and showed the giant his belt. "Read there what sort of man I am."

The giant read, "Seven at one stroke." He of course thought that it was seven men that the tailor had killed at one stroke and decided that he should be a little careful with the small, strange fellow. "I know," thought the giant, "I'll find out how strong he is." He picked up a stone and crushed it in his large hands until water came out of it.

"If you really have any strength you will be able to do the same."

"That is child's play for someone like me," replied the little tailor. He took the cheese out of his pocket and crushed it until it was wet through.

The giant did not know what to say but he was still doubtful of the little man's power, so he picked up another stone and threw it so high that it almost went out of sight.

"Now," he said, "you do that!"

"Well thrown, I'll give you that," replied the tailor, "but your stone fell to earth again. I will throw one that won't come down again."

He took the bird from his pocket and threw it into the air. The bird, happy to be free, was quick to fly high into the sky and was soon out of sight. "There what do you think of that, my friend?" asked the tailor.

"Well, I agree that you can throw, but now I'll see if you can carry a heavy weight," answered the giant.

He led the little tailor to a mighty tree that had fallen and lay on the ground. "If you are strong enough, help me carry this out of the wood."

"With pleasure," said the little man. "You take the trunk on your shoulder, and I will carry the branches, which is the most difficult part."

The giant took the trunk on his shoulders, and the tailor seated himself on a branch. As the giant could not look around, he had to carry not only the whole tree, but the tailor as well.

The little man was really enjoying himself and even started singing one of his favorite songs, as if carrying a tree was the easiest thing in the world.

The giant, after he had carried the heavy tree some distance, was out of breath and called out that he must stop and rest.

The tailor jumped off, caught hold of the tree with both arms as if he had been carrying it all the way and said to the giant, "To think that a big fellow like you can't even carry a tree!"

They walked on together until they came to a fruit tree. The giant quickly took hold of the top of the tree, where the sweetest fruit grew and pulled it towards the ground. He told the tailor to eat as much fruit as he wanted and put the tree in the little man's hands. When the giant let go, the tailor was too weak to hold it, and the tree, springing back into the air, carried the tailor with it.

When he jumped unhurt to the ground, the giant cried, "Didn't you have enough strength to hold that small tree?"

"It has nothing to do with strength, my dear fellow, do you suppose that I, who have killed seven at one stroke, could not have done it? I jumped over the tree simply because I saw a hunter about to take a shot at me. Jump it yourself, if you can."

The giant made an attempt but could not clear the tree and found himself caught up in the branches, so once again the little tailor got the best of him.

When he had got down the giant said, "As you are such a brave fellow, come and stay with us tonight."

The tailor followed the giant to his home where he saw many other giants. They were sitting around a fire eating large amounts of food, and they looked at the tailor as though they would eat him too. Then the giant showed him a bed and told him to lie down and rest. The bed was too big for the tailor so he went over to one side and slept in a corner.

In the middle of the night, when the giant thought that the tailor was asleep, he took an iron nail and drove it into the middle of the bed, and thought he had made an end of the objectionable little man.

At break of day, the giants went out into the woods thinking that the tailor was dead. A little later, however, the tailor came walking towards them as lively and happy as ever. The giants then became very afraid, and they thought the tailor would kill them so they ran away as fast as they could. The tailor, who knew nothing of the attempt on his life, thought that this was rather strange of the giants, but decided to continue on his journey to see the world.

After walking for some time he came to a large palace and he decided to rest before entering. As he lay sleeping on the ground, people came out of the palace to look at him. They read what was written on his belt, "Seven at one stroke!"

"Ah!" they thought, "this must be a great soldier." Some of them went to the king and told him of the "great soldier," saying that if a war broke out he would be a very useful man to have around.

The king thought this was a good idea and sent one of his men to offer the "great soldier" a position in the army. The man watched over the sleeping tailor and, when he opened his eyes, made the offer.

"This was the reason I came here," answered the tailor. "I am ready to enter the king's service."

He was received with great honor and given a special house to live in. The other soldiers in the king's army, however, did not like the tailor. They were afraid that if he got angry with them he could kill seven of them with each stroke. So they all went to the king together and resigned because of the tailor.

The king was sorry to lose all his soldiers because of one man. But he too was afraid of the tailor and did not want to tell him to go. So he tried to think of a plan to remove the tailor from his kingdom without making him angry. He thought for a long time; then at last he hit on a plan. He sent for the little tailor and told him a story.

In a certain wood in his kingdom lived two giants. Everyone was afraid of them because they took money off of anybody they met and killed anyone who tried to stand up to them. The king told the tailor that if he overcame and killed the giants he would give him the hand of his only daughter in marriage and half his kingdom.

The little tailor did not take too long to think about it.

"Of course I will do it. It is not every day that you get offered a beautiful princess and half a kingdom. A man who can kill seven at a stroke is more than a match for two."

The next day the tailor set off. When he reached the wood, he started looking for the giants. After a while, he saw them sleeping under a tree. The little tailor quickly filled his pockets with stones and went up the tree. When he was on the branch immediately above the giants, he started to drop stones on one of them. For a long time the giant did not move but when he did wake up he pushed his companion and asked, "Why are you hitting me?"

"You're dreaming," replied the other giant, "I didn't hit you."

Again they lay down to sleep, and again

the little tailor dropped a stone, this time on the second giant.

"What's that?" cried the giant, "Why are you hitting me?"

"I am not hitting you," answered the first giant in an angry voice, "now stop waking me up." After a few angry words they settled down to try to sleep. The little tailor renewed his game, picked his biggest stone and dropped it on the head of the first giant.

"This is too much," shouted the giant and he jumped up like a madman. He picked up his companion and pushed him back against the tree with such force that the tailor had to hold on with both hands to stop himself from falling out. With one powerful blow the second giant knocked the first one to the floor and then a mighty fight took place. The giants pulled up trees and hit each other over the head until at last they both lay dead on the ground.

The tailor quickly jumped down from his tree, drew his sword and pushed it into the body of each of the giants. He then called out to the servants who had accompanied him as far as the wood, to come and see what he had done. The servants could hardly believe their eyes; there were fallen trees everywhere and, lying side by side in their own blood, were the two giants.

When he returned to the palace he demanded that the king fulfill his promise. But the king tried to think of a way to put him off.

"Before you win my daughter and half of my kingdom I require you to do another great act. You must catch a dangerous unicorn that is wild in the wood."

"I am even less afraid of unicorns than I am of giants," said the tailor.

Once again he entered the wood leaving

his servants outside. He quickly saw the unicorn, which made straight for him. He stood quite still, and, when the unicorn charged him, he jumped quickly behind a tree. The unicorn could not stop and hit the tree so hard that its horn got stuck in it.

"Now I have you," said the tailor and he cut off the unicorn's horn with his sword. Without its sharp horn the unicorn was no longer dangerous, and the tailor was able to lead the animal peacefully back to the king.

But the king still did not keep his promise. "Before we set a date for the wedding you must catch one last wild animal still free in the wood. It's a danger to everyone."

"I will go with pleasure," said the tailor; "hunting this animal will be child's play for me."

When the animal saw the tailor it rushed at him angrily ready to knock him over. The tailor was too quick for him, however, and ran into an old house that was nearby. When the animal rushed in after him, the tailor jumped out of the window, ran round the house and closed the door. The angry animal tried to get through the window but was far too heavy and ended up lying unhappily on the floor.

After his latest success the tailor returned to the king and demanded that he honor his promise. The king had no choice and the wedding went ahead although both he and his daughter, the princess, were unhappy. The tailor was, of course, very happy; he was now a king with a beautiful wife.

Soon afterwards the new queen heard her husband talking in his sleep one night. He was talking about his old job and speaking about the clothes he had made. She then realized what her husband had been before he came to her father's kingdom. Not a "great soldier," but a simple tailor! The next morning she went to her father and told him that he had married her off to a poor tailor.

The old king thought about it for a moment then replied, "Tonight leave your bedroom door open; when he is asleep my soldiers will come in, tie him up and put him on a ship that will take him to the other side of the world."

However, the tailor's servant, and only real friend, had heard this plan and told his master what the old king wanted to do.

"Don't worry," said the tailor, "I'll stop their little plan."

That night he went to bed at the same time as usual and lay down by his wife. When his wife thought he was asleep, she got up and opened the door. Almost at once the tailor started talking, but this time he was not really asleep. "I have killed seven at one stroke, killed two giants, caught a unicorn and a wild animal; is it likely that I would be afraid of someone waiting outside my bedroom?"

When the soldiers heard the tailor talking like this, they became very fearful, and instead of tying him up they ran away. From then on nobody ever dared to lay a finger on him. The brave little tailor remained king to the end of his days.

The Golden Goose

読みはじめる前に

　The Golden Goose で使われている用語です。わからない語は巻末のワードリストで確認しましょう。

- [ ] bystander
- [ ] churchman
- [ ] condition
- [ ] force
- [ ] government
- [ ] hunger
- [ ] spare

登場人物

Dunderhead　ぬけ作　3人兄弟の末っ子。心優しいが親兄弟から馬鹿にされ、冷たくされている。

eldest brother　長男　ぬけ作の兄。思いやりがない。

second son　次男　ぬけ作の兄。長男同様、思いやりがない。

gray-haired old man　白髪頭の老人　やさしくしてくれたお礼に、ぬけ作に金のがちょうを与える。

landlord of the house　宿屋の主人　ぬけ作が泊まる宿の主人。娘が3人いる。

king　王様　まったく笑わない娘を心配し、娘を笑わせた男を娘と結婚させると発表する。

Once there was a man who had three sons. The youngest, called Dunderhead, was thought to be a fool by the other two sons. They were always telling him how foolish he was and generally made his life unpleasant.

One day the eldest brother wanted to go into the forest to cut some wood. Before he left, his mother gave him a freshly cooked cake and a bottle of wine to take for his dinner. On the edge of the forest he met a gray-haired old man, who wished him good day and asked for a piece of the cake and some wine, as he had not had food or drink for some time.

The son answered, "Why should I give you my cake and wine? I would have less myself. Be off with you."

He continued into the forest leaving

the gray-haired old man behind him. He started cutting wood but soon made a bad stroke and hit his arm, and he was forced to return home to rest.

The second son then went into the forest and his mother gave him some cake and wine. He too passed the old man, who asked for some food. "Get your own food, old man," replied the second son, "Why should I give you mine?" He then started to cut wood but before long had hit his own leg and had to be carried home.

Then Dunderhead asked his father if he could go and cut wood.

"Look what happened to the other two when they went. You, who have no sense, had better not go to the forest."

But Dunderhead kept asking his father until at last he was allowed to go. Instead of cake and wine his mother gave him some dry bread and water. As he was entering the forest, the gray-haired old man came up to him and asked him for food and something to drink. Dunderhead replied, "Sit down my good fellow, I only have bread and water, but you are welcome to share that with me." When he tasted his food, Dunderhead found that his dry bread had turned into a lovely cake and the water had become wine.

After they had shared the meal, the old man said, "Because you have a kind heart and have shared your meal with me, I will do you a good turn. Over there stands an old tree; cut it down, and you will find something worth having in the trunk."

Dunderhead cut the tree down, and as it hit the ground a golden goose fell out. He picked it up and went into town and took a room for the night.

The landlord of the house where he was staying had three daughters. As soon as they saw the wonderful goose they wanted to have it. When Dunderhead left his room, the eldest daughter went quietly in and picked up the goose. Straight away she realized something was wrong as she could not get her hands free. She called out to her sisters that she was stuck fast and they rushed in to help her. Before long they too were sticking to the goose and ended up having to pass the night with it.

The next morning, Dunderhead took his goose and left, saying nothing to the three girls sticking to it. They were forced to run along behind him. In the middle of the field they passed a well-known churchman and when he saw the group he shouted at the girls, "What are you doing running after a man like that? It's not right, wait till I tell your father." When the girls continued running behind Dunderhead and the goose, he ran after them and caught hold of the youngest. Straight away he was caught fast, unable to free himself and found himself having to run along behind the girls.

A little way along the road they passed a friend of the churchman, a very important member of the town government. When he saw his friend running after the girls, he said, "What are you doing? Think of what this looks like. A man of your age and position running after three young girls."

As they passed by, he tried to pull the churchman off but he, too, was soon being pulled through the town behind Dunderhead and the goose. As they went along, they passed two workmen and the churchman shouted at them to set them free, but no sooner had the workmen touched one of the group than they too became stuck fast and had to follow where Dunderhead led.

They then came to a town where a king lived. This king had a daughter who was so unhappy that she never laughed. The king had made it known that whoever succeeded in making her laugh could marry her.

Dunderhead took his group past her. As soon as she saw everybody sticking to each other, running behind the goose, she started laughing. As he had made the unhappy princess laugh for the first time, Dunderhead asked for her hand in marriage. The king, however, did not really want Dunderhead as a son-in-law and quickly added another condition to be fulfilled before he could marry her. This time Dunderhead must find a man who could drink twelve bottles of wine at one sitting.

Dunderhead thought about the gray-haired old man who had helped him before and went back to the forest to look for him. He found the little man sitting under a tree looking very unhappy.

"What's up?" asked Dunderhead.

"Well," replied the old man, "I haven't had a good drink for many days and I am as dry as a bone. I feel like I could drink a whole lake of wine."

"Come with me, my friend," said Dunderhead, "I've got just the thing for you!"

He led him back to the king's palace and to the great surprise of everyone, the gray-haired old man not only drank the twelve bottles but asked for more!

Dunderhead once more asked to marry the daughter but the king set a new condition. This time a man had to be found who could eat a mountain of bread. Once again Dunderhead returned to the forest and found the gray-haired old man sitting under the same tree looking tired and thin.

"What's wrong, my friend, you don't look well at all?"

"I have a hunger that I cannot get rid of," replied the old man, "No matter how much I eat, I do not feel full up."

"Maybe I can help," said Dunderhead and led him back to the king's palace.

Although it seemed like all the bread in the kingdom had been brought to the palace, the old man sat down and started eating. Within an hour there was nothing left, and he left the palace asking the bystanders if they had any spare food for a hungry old man.

Even then the king would not agree to the marriage but told Dunderhead that he must bring to the palace a ship that could sail on land as well as water. "If you do this one last thing," said the king, "You shall have my daughter's hand in marriage."

Right away Dunderhead set off for the forest. He found the old man and told him of the king's last condition.

"Because you were so kind to me before, I will help you again," said the gray-haired old man.

He quickly built a ship that could sail on both land and sea, and Dunderhead sailed in it to the palace. When the king saw it, he knew he could not put Dunderhead off any longer and agreed to the marriage.

The people of the kingdom had grown to like Dunderhead as he answered the conditions laid down by the king, and they were full of joy when the pair got married. Dunderhead went on to live a long and happy life and succeeded to the throne when the old king died.

Word List

- LEVEL 1、2は本文で使われている全ての語を掲載しています。
  LEVEL 3以上は、中学校レベルの語を含みません。ただし、本文で特殊な意味で使われている場合、その意味のみを掲載しています。
- 語形が規則変化する語の見出しは原形で示しています。不規則変化語は本文中で使われている形になっています。
- 一般的な意味を紹介していますので、一部の語で本文で実際に使われている品詞や意味と合っていないことがあります。
- 品詞は以下のように示しています。

名 名詞	代 代名詞	形 形容詞	副 副詞	動 動詞	助 助動詞
前 前置詞	接 接続詞	間 間投詞	冠 冠詞	略 略語	俗 俗語
熟 熟語	頭 接頭語	尾 接尾語	記 記号	関 関係代名詞	

A

- □ **a** 冠 ①1つの、1人の、ある ②~につき
- □ **a.m.** 《A.M. とも》午前
- □ **able** 形 ①《be - to ~》(人が)~することができる ②能力のある
- □ **about** 前 ①~について ②~のまわりに[の]
- □ **above** 前 ~の上に
- □ **accompany** 動 ついていく、つきそう
- □ **across** 前 ~を渡って、~の向こう側に
- □ **act** 名 行為、行い 動 ①行動する ②演じる
- □ **add** 動 加える、足す
- □ **afraid** 形 ①心配して、恐れて、こわがって be afraid of ~を恐れる、~を怖がる
- □ **after** 前 ①~の後に[で]、~の次に ②《前後に名詞がきて》次々に~、何度も~《反復・継続を表す》after a while しばらくして look after ~の世話をする、~に気をつける 副 後に[で]
- □ **afterwards** 副 その後、のちに
- □ **again** 副 再び、もう一度 again and again 何度も繰り返して

- □ **against** 前 ①~に対して、~に反対して、(規則など)に違反して ②~にもたれて against the wall 壁を背にして
- □ **age** 名 年齢
- □ **agree** 動 ①同意する ②意見が一致する
- □ **ah** 間 《驚き・悲しみ・賞賛などを表して》ああ、やっぱり
- □ **ahead** 副 前方へ[に] ahead of ~より先[前]に、~に先んじて go ahead 先に行く、《許可を表す》どうぞ
- □ **air** 名 《the -》空中、空間
- □ **all** 形 すべての、~中 all day 一日中、明けても暮れても all day long 一日中、終日 all kinds of さまざまな、あらゆる種類の all one's life ずっと、生まれてから all the way ずっと、はるばる、いろいろと 代 全部、すべて(のもの[人]) not at all 少しも~でない not ~ at all 少しも[全然]~ない 副 まったく、すっかり
- □ **allow** 動 ①許す、《- - to ~》…が~するのを可能にする、…に~させておく ②与える
- □ **almost** 副 ほとんど、もう少しで(~するところ)
- □ **alone** 副 ひとりで、~だけで leave

Word List

~ alone ~をそっとしておく
- **along** 前 ~に沿って **go along ~**に沿って行く, (人)について行く 副 ~に沿って, 前へ, 進んで **come along** ①一緒に来る, ついて来る ②やって来る, 現れる ③うまくいく, よくなる, できあがる
- **already** 副 すでに, もう
- **also** 接 その上, さらに
- **although** 接 ~だけれども, ~にもかかわらず, たとえ~でも
- **always** 副 いつも, 常に
- **am** 動 ~である, (~に)いる[ある]《主語がIのときのbeの現在形》
- **among** 前 (3つ以上のもの)の間で[に], ~の中で[に]
- **amount** 名 ①量, 額 ②《the -》合計
- **an** 冠 ①1つの, 1人の, ある ②~につき
- **and** 接 ①そして, ~と… ②《同じ語を結んで》ますます ③《結果を表して》それで, だから
- **anger** 名 怒り
- **angrily** 副 怒って, 腹立たしげに
- **angry** 形 怒って, 腹を立てて **get angry** 腹を立てる
- **angry-looking** 形 怒っているような
- **animal** 名 動物
- **announcement** 名 発表, アナウンス, 告示, 声明
- **another** 形 ①もう1つ[1人]の ②別の
- **answer** 動 答える, 応じる 名 答え, 応答, 返事
- **any** 形 ①《疑問文で》何か, いくつかの ②《否定文で》何も 少しも(~ない) ③《肯定文で》どの~も **any better** 少しでもよい **in any way** 決して, 多少なりとも 代 ①《疑問文で》(~のうち)何か, どれか, 誰か ②《否定文で》少しも, 何も[誰も]~ない ③《肯定文で》どれも, 誰でも
- **anybody** 代 ①《疑問文・条件節で》誰か ②《否定文で》誰も(~ない) ③《肯定文で》誰でも
- **anymore** 副 《通例否定文, 疑問文で》今はもう, これ以上, これから
- **anyone** 代 ①《疑問文・条件節で》誰か ②《否定文で》誰も(~ない) ③《肯定文で》誰でも
- **anything** 代 ①《疑問文で》何か, どれでも ②《否定文で》何も, どれも(~ない) ③《肯定文で》何でも, どれでも **anything else** ほかの何か
- **anyway** 副 ①いずれにせよ, ともかく ②どんな方法でも
- **anywhere** 副 どこかへ[に], どこにも, どこへも, どこにでも
- **appear** 動 ①現れる, 見えてくる ②(~のように)見える, ~らしい
- **are** 動 ~である, (~に)いる[ある]《主語がyou, we, theyまたは複数名詞のときのbeの現在形》
- **arm** 名 腕
- **army** 名 軍隊
- **around** 副 ①まわりに, あちこちに ②およそ, 約 **look around** まわりを見回す 前 ~のまわりに, ~のあちこちに
- **arrive** 動 ①~に到着する ②~に到達する **arrive at** ~に着く
- **as** 接 ①《as ~ as …の形で》…と同じくらい~ ②~のとおりに, ~のように ③~しながら, ~しているときに ④~につれて, ~にしたがって ⑤~なので ⑥~だけれども ⑦~する限りでは 前 ①~として(の) ②~の時 副 同じくらい~ **as A so B** AとBと同様にB **as dry as a bone** 骨のように干からびた, 乾ききった **as ever** 相変わらず, これまでのように **as far as** ~と同じくらい遠く, ~まで, ~する限り(では) **as far as one can** できるだけ **as if** あたかも~のように, まるで~みたいに **as soon as** ~するとすぐ, ~するや否や **as though** あたかも~のように, まるで~みたいに **as usual** いつものように, 相変わらず **as well** なお, その上,

The Best of Grimm's Fairy Tales

- 同様に **as well as** 〜と同様に **as 〜 as ever** 相変わらず, これまでのように **as 〜 as one can** できる限り〜 **the same 〜 as** ……と同じ(ような)
- **ask** 動 ①尋ねる, 聞く ②頼む, 求める **ask 〜 if** 〜かどうか尋ねる
- **asleep** 形 眠って(いる状態の) **fall asleep** 眠り込む, 寝入る 副 眠って, 休止して
- **at** 前 ①《場所・時》〜に[で] ②《目標・方向》〜に[を], 〜に向かって ③《原因・理由》〜を見て[聞いて・知って] ④〜に従事して, 〜の状態で
- **ate** 動 eat (食べる)の過去
- **attempt** 動 試みる, 企てる 名 試み, 企て, 努力
- **aunt** 名 おば
- **awake** 動 ①目覚めさせる ②目覚める 形 目が覚めて
- **away** 副 離れて, 遠くに, 去って, わきに **far away** 遠く離れて
- **awoke** 動 awake (目覚めさせる)の過去
- **ax** 名 おの

B

- **back** 副 ①戻って ②後ろへ[に] **come back** 戻る **come back for** 〜の目的で戻って来る **get back** 戻る, 帰る **get 〜 back** 〜を取り返す[戻す] **go back to** 〜に帰る[戻る], 〜に遡る, (中断していた作業に)再び取り掛かる **look back at** 〜に視線を戻す, 〜を振り返って見る **push back** 押し返す, 押しのける **put back** (もとの場所に)戻す, 返す 形 裏の, 後ろの
- **back door** 裏口, 勝手口
- **bad** 形 悪い, へたな, まずい **make a bad stroke** (おのを)下ろし損ねる
- **bag** 名 袋, かばん
- **ball** 名 ボール, 球
- **bank** 名 岸
- **barely** 副 かろうじて, やっと
- **be** 動 〜である, (〜に)いる[ある], 〜となる 助 《現在分詞とともに用いて》〜している ①《過去分詞とともに用いて》〜される, 〜されている
- **beautiful** 形 美しい, すばらしい
- **beautifully** 副 美しく, 立派に, 見事に
- **became** 動 become (なる)の過去
- **because** 接 (なぜなら)〜だから, 〜という理由[原因]で **because of** 〜のために, 〜の理由で
- **become** 動 ①(〜に)なる ② becomeの過去分詞 **become stuck** (異物が)詰まる
- **bed** 名 ベッド, 寝所 **get into bed** ベッドに入る **go to bed** 床につく, 寝る **head of the bead** ベッドの頭の方
- **bedroom** 名 寝室
- **bedtime** 名 就寝の時刻
- **been** 動 be (〜である)の過去分詞 **have been to** 〜へ行ったことがある 助 be (〜している・〜される)の過去分詞
- **before** 前 〜の前に[で], 〜より以前に 接 〜する前に 副 以前に **before long** やがて, まもなく **the day before** 前日 **the night before** 前の晩
- **began** 動 begin (始まる)の過去
- **behind** 前 ①〜の後ろに, 〜の背後に ②〜に遅れて, 〜に劣って 副 ①後ろに, 背後に ②遅れて, 劣って
- **believe** 動 信じる, 信じている, (〜と)思う, 考える
- **below** 前 〜より下に
- **belt** 名 ベルト, バンド
- **beside** 前 〜のそばに, 〜と並んで
- **best** 形 最もよい, 最大[多]の 名 《the -》①最上のもの ②全力, 精いっぱい **get the best of** 〜を負かす, 出し抜く

Word List

- **better** 形 ①よりよい ②(人が)回復して **get better** (病気などが)良くなる 副 ①よりよく、より上手に ②むしろ **any better** 少しでもよい **had better** 〜したほうが身のためだ、〜しなさい

- **beyond** 前 〜を越えて、〜の向こうに 副 向こうに

- **big** 形 ①大きい ②偉い、重要な

- **bird** 名 鳥

- **black** 形 黒い、有色の 名 黒、黒色

- **blew** 動 blow (吹く)の過去

- **blood** 名 血、血液

- **blow** 動 (風が)吹く 名 打撃

- **blue** 形 青い 名 青(色)

- **boat** 名 ボート、小舟、船

- **body** 名 体、死体、胴体

- **bone** 名 骨 **as dry as a bone** 骨のように干からびた、乾ききった

- **borrow** 動 借りる、借金する

- **both** 形 両方の、2つとも 副 《both 〜 and … の形で》〜も…も両方とも 代 両方、両者、双方 **both of them** 彼ら[それら]両方とも

- **bottle** 名 瓶、ボトル

- **bottled** 形 瓶詰めの

- **bottom** 名 底、下部

- **boy** 名 少年、男の子

- **branch** 名 枝

- **brave** 形 勇敢な

- **bread** 名 パン

- **break** 動 壊す、折る **break out** 発生する、急に起こる、(戦争が)勃発する 名 破壊、割れ目 **at break of day** 夜明けに

- **breath** 名 息、呼吸 **out of breath** 息を切らして

- **breathe** 動 呼吸する

- **bright** 形 輝いている、鮮明な

- **brightly** 副 明るく、輝いて、快活に

- **bring** 動 持ってくる、連れてくる

- **broke** 動 break (壊す)の過去

- **broken** 動 break (壊す)の過去分詞 形 ①破れた、壊れた ②落胆した

- **brother** 名 兄弟

- **brought** 動 bring (持ってくる)の過去、過去分詞

- **built** 動 build (建てる)の過去、過去分詞 **be built of** 〜で造られている

- **burn** 動 燃える

- **but** 接 ①でも、しかし ②〜を除いて **not only 〜 but (also) …** 〜だけでなく…もまた **not 〜 but …** 〜ではなくて… 前 〜を除いて、〜のほかは 副 ただ、のみ、ほんの

- **buy** 動 買う、獲得する

- **by** 前 ①《位置》〜のそばに[で] ②《手段・方法・行為者・基準》〜によって、〜で ③《期限》〜までには ④《通過・経由》〜を経由して、〜を通って 副 そばに、通り過ぎて

- **bystander** 名 傍観者、見物人

C

- **cake** 名 菓子、ケーキ

- **call** 動 呼ぶ、叫ぶ **call for** 〜を求める、訴える、〜を呼び求める、呼び出す **call out** 叫ぶ、呼び出す、声を掛ける **call to** 〜に声をかける

- **came** 動 come (来る)の過去

- **can** 助 ①〜できる ②〜してもよい ③〜でありうる ④《否定文で》〜のはずがない **as far as one can** できるだけ **as 〜 as one can** できる限り〜 **can hardly** とても〜できない **Can you 〜?** 〜してくれますか。

- **cannot** can (〜できる)の否定形 (=can not)

- **care** 名 ①心配、注意 ②世話、介護 **take care** 気をつける、注意する **take care of** 〜の世話をする、〜面倒を見る、〜を管理する

- **careful** 形 注意深い、慎重な

The Best of Grimm's Fairy Tales

- **carriage** 名馬車
- **carry** 動運ぶ, 連れていく, 持ち歩く **carry out** 外へ運び出す
- **catch** 動つかまえる **catch hold of** ～をつかむ, 捕らえる **catch on** ～にぶつける, ～に引っかかる **catch up with** ～に追いつく
- **caught** 動catch (つかまえる)の過去, 過去分詞
- **cause** 動(～の)原因となる, 引き起こす
- **certain** 形ある
- **chair** 名いす
- **chance** 名①偶然, 運 ②好機 **take a chance** いちかばちかやってみる
- **change** 動変わる, 変える 名変化, 変更 **for a change** 気分転換に
- **charge** 動突進する
- **cheese** 名チーズ
- **child** 名子ども **child's play** 非常に簡単なこと, 朝飯前のこと
- **children** 名child (子ども)の複数
- **choice** 名選択(の範囲・自由)
- **chose** 動choose (選ぶ)の過去
- **churchman** 名聖職者, 牧師
- **city** 名都市, 都会
- **clean** 形きれいな, 清潔な
- **clear** 形①はっきりした, 明白な ②澄んだ ③(よく)晴れた 動(障害物を)飛び越える, 通過する
- **climb** 動登る, 徐々に上がる
- **close** 形①近い ②親しい ③狭い **close by** すぐ近くに **get close to** ～に近づく, 接近する 副①接近して ②密集して 動①閉まる, 閉める ②終える, 閉店する
- **closed** 動close (閉まる)の過去, 過去分詞 形閉じた, 閉鎖した
- **cloth** 名布(地), テーブルクロス, ふきん
- **clothes** 名衣服, 身につけるもの

- **coat** 名①コート ②(動物の)毛
- **coin** 名硬貨, コイン
- **cold** 形寒い, 冷たい
- **college** 名(単科)大学
- **colored** 形①色のついた ②有色人種の, 黒人の
- **come** 動①来る, 行く, 現れる ②(出来事が)起こる, 生じる ③～になる ④comeの過去分詞 **come along** ①一緒に来る, ついて来る ②やって来る, 現れる ③うまくいく, よくなる, できあがる **come and** ～しに行く **come back** 戻る **come back for** ～の目的で戻って来る **come by** やって来る, 立ち寄る **come down** ～を下りて来る **come for** ～の目的で来る, ～を取りに来る **come in** 中にはいる, やってくる, 出回る **come on** ①いいかげんにしろ, もうよせ, さあ来なさい ②(人)に偶然出合う **come out** 出てくる, 出掛ける, 姿を現す, 発行される **come out of** ～から出てくる, ～をうまく乗り越える **come over** やって来る, ～の身にふりかかる **come over to** ～にやって来る **come true** 実現する **come up** 近づいてくる, 階上に行く **how come** どうして, なぜ
- **companion** 名友, 仲間, 連れ
- **complete** 動完成させる
- **condition** 名条件
- **contain** 動含む, 入っている
- **continue** 動続く, 続ける
- **control** 動管理[支配]する
- **cook** 動料理する, (食べ物が)煮える
- **cooked** 形加熱調理した
- **cool** 形涼しい, 冷えた
- **coolly** 副冷静に, 冷たく
- **corner** 名すみ, はずれ
- **cost** 名値段, 費用
- **could** 動①can (～できる)の過去 ②《控え目な推量・可能性・願望などを表す》**could have done** ～だったかもしれない《仮定法》**Could I ～?** ～してもよいですか。 **How could**

WORD LIST

～? 何だって～なんてことがありえようか? **If**＋《主語》＋**could** ～できればなあ《仮定法》

- [ ] **country** 名 ①国 ②(the -)田舎, 郊外 形 田舎の
- [ ] **countryside** 名 地方, 田舎
- [ ] **couple** 名 ①2つ, 対 ②夫婦, 一組
- [ ] **course** 名 ①進路, 方向 ②経過, 成り行き ③科目, 講座 ④策, 方案 **of course** もちろん, 当然
- [ ] **cover** 動 扱う, (～に)わたる, 及ぶ
- [ ] **crown** 名 冠
- [ ] **crush** 動 押しつぶす, 砕く, 粉々にする
- [ ] **cry** 動 泣く, 叫ぶ, 大声を出す, 嘆く **cry out** 叫ぶ
- [ ] **crying** 名 泣き叫び
- [ ] **cut** 動 ①切る, 刈る ②短縮する, 削る ③cutの過去, 過去分詞 **cut down** 切り倒す, 打ちのめす **cut off** 切断する, 切り離す **cut out** 切り取る, 切り抜く 名 切ること, 切り傷

D

- [ ] **dance** 動 踊る, ダンスをする 名 ダンス, ダンスパーティー
- [ ] **dancing** 名 ダンス, 舞踏
- [ ] **danger** 名 危険, 障害, 脅威
- [ ] **dangerous** 形 危険な, 有害な
- [ ] **dare** 動《 to ～》思い切って[あえて]～する
- [ ] **dark** 形 ①暗い, 闇の ②(色が)濃い, (髪が)黒い ③陰うつな
- [ ] **date** 名 日付, 年月日 **set a date** 日取りを決める
- [ ] **daughter** 名 娘
- [ ] **dawn** 名 夜明け
- [ ] **day** 名 ①日中, 昼間 ②日, 期日 ③《-s》時代, 生涯 **all day** 一日中, 明けても暮れても **all day long** 一日中, 終日 **at break of day** 夜明けに **every day** 毎日 **good day** こんにちは **one day**（過去の）ある日,（未来の）いつか **take the rest of the day off** 今日はもう帰る **the day before** 前日 **wish someone good day**（人）の一日の幸運を祈る

- [ ] **dead** 形 死んでいる **lie dead** 死んで横たわっている
- [ ] **dear** 形 いとしい, 親愛なる, 大事な 名 ねえ, あなた《呼びかけ》
- [ ] **decide** 動 決定[決意]する,（～しようと）決める, 判決を下す
- [ ] **deep** 形 深い
- [ ] **deer** 名 シカ(鹿)
- [ ] **delighted** 形 喜んでいる, うれしそうな
- [ ] **demand** 動 要求する
- [ ] **did** 動 do（～をする）の過去 助 doの過去
- [ ] **die** 動 死ぬ, 消滅する **die of** ～がもとで死ぬ
- [ ] **difficult** 形 困難な, むずかしい, 扱いにくい
- [ ] **dinner** 名 ①ディナー, 夕食 ②夕食[食事]会, 祝宴
- [ ] **dinner-time** 名 夕食の時間
- [ ] **disappear** 動 見えなくなる, 姿を消す, なくなる
- [ ] **dish** 名 ①大皿 ②料理
- [ ] **distance** 名 距離, 隔たり, 遠方
- [ ] **do** 助 ①《ほかの動詞とともに用いて現在形の否定文・疑問文をつくる》②《同じ動詞を繰り返す代わりに用いる》③《動詞を強調するのに用いる》動 ～をする **do with** ～を処理する **do ～ a good turn** ～を助ける
- [ ] **doctor** 名 医者
- [ ] **does** 動 do（～をする）の3人称単数現在 助 doの3人称単数現在
- [ ] **dog** 名 犬
- [ ] **dollar** 名 ①ドル《米国などの通貨単位。記号 $ 》②《-s》金銭
- [ ] **done** 動 do（～をする）の過去分詞
- [ ] **door** 名 ドア, 戸

THE BEST OF GRIMM'S FAIRY TALES

- **doubtful** 形 疑わしい, あやふやな, おぼつかない, (人物が)いかがわしい be doubtful of ～を疑う
- **down** 副 ①下へ, 降りて, 低くなって ②倒れて 前 ～の下方へ, ～を下って 形 下方の, 下りの
- **drank** 動 drink (飲む)の過去
- **dream** 名 夢, 幻想 動 (～の)夢を見る, 夢想[想像]する
- **dress** 名 ドレス, 衣服, 正装 動 ①服を着る[着せる] ②飾る
- **drew** 動 draw (引く)の過去
- **drink** 動 飲む, 飲酒する 名 飲み物, 酒, 1杯 good drink 旨い酒
- **drive** 動 ①車で行く, (車を)運転する ②追いやる, (ある状態に)する drive away (虫などを)追い払う
- **drop** 動 ①(ぽたぽた)落ちる, 落とす ②下がる, 下げる drop out of ～からこぼれ落ちる 名 しずく, 落下
- **drove** 動 drive (車で行く)の過去
- **drunk** 動 drink (飲む)の過去分詞
- **dry** 形 ①乾燥した ②辛口の as dry as a bone 骨のように干からびた, 乾ききった
- **Dunderhead** 名 ぬけ作《愛称》

E

- **each** 形 それぞれの, 各自の, お互いに each time ～するたびに 代 それぞれ, 各自 each other 副 それぞれに
- **early** 形 ①(時間や時期が)早い ②初期の, 幼少の, 若い 副 ①早く, 早めに ②初期に, 初めのころに
- **earth** 名 ①《the ～》地球 ②大地, 陸地, 土 ③この世
- **easy** 形 ①やさしい, 簡単な ②気楽な, くつろいだ
- **eat** 動 食べる, 食事する eat off ～から食べる eat out of ～から取って食べる
- **eaten** 動 eat (食べる)の過去分詞
- **edge** 名 ①刃 ②端, 縁
- **eight** 名 8(の数字), 8人[個] 形 8の, 8人[個]の
- **either** 形 ①(2つのうち)どちらかの ②どちらでも either side of ～の両側に on either side 両側に 副 ①どちらか ②《否定文で》～もまた(…ない)
- **eldest** 形 最年長の
- **else** 副 ①そのほかに[の], 代わりに ②さもないと anything else ほかの何か
- **empty** 形 ①空の, 空いている ②(心などが)ぼんやりした, 無意味な 動 空になる[する], 注ぐ
- **end** 名 ①終わり, 終末, 死 ②果て, 末, 端 ③目的 make an end of ～をおしまいにする 動 終わる, 終える end up 結局～になる
- **enjoy** 動 楽しむ, 享受する enjoy oneself 楽しく過ごす, 楽しむ
- **enough** 形 十分な, (～するに)足る enough to do ～するのに十分な 代 十分(な量・数), たくさん 副 (～できる)だけ, 十分に, まったく
- **enter** 動 入る, 入会[入学]する[させる]
- **escape** 動 逃げる, 免れる, もれる
- **even** 副 ①《強意》～でさえも, ～すら, いっそう, なおさら ②平等に even if たとえ～でも even then その時でさえ even though ～であるけれども, ～にもかかわらず 形 ①平らな, 水平の ②等しい, 均一の ③落ち着いた 動 平らになる[する], 釣り合いがとれる
- **evening** 名 夕方, 晩
- **ever** 副 ①今までに, これまで, かつて, いつまでも ②《強意》いったい as ever 相変わらず, これまでのように as ～ as ever 相変わらず, これまでのように
- **every** 形 ①どの～も, すべての, あらゆる ②毎～, ～ごとの every day 毎日 every time ～するときはいつ

WORD LIST

- **everybody** 代誰でも, 皆
- **everyone** 代誰でも, 皆
- **everything** 代すべてのこと[もの], 何でも, 何もかも make everything right 全てうまくいかせる
- **everywhere** 副どこにいても, いたるところに
- **except** 前~を除いて, ~のほかは
- **eye** 名目

F

- **face** 名顔, 顔つき 動直面する
- **fact** 名事実, 真相 in fact つまり, 実は, 要するに
- **fail** 動失敗する
- **faithful** 形忠実な, 正確な
- **fall** 動①落ちる, 倒れる ②(ある状態に)急に陥る fall asleep 眠り込む, 寝入る fall into ~に陥る, ~してしまう fall out 落ちる, 飛び出す fall to the ground 転ぶ 名①落下, 墜落 ②滝 ③崩壊 ④秋
- **fallen** 動 fall (落ちる)の過去分詞 形落ちた, 倒れた
- **family** 名家族, 家庭, 一門, 家柄
- **famous** 形有名な, 名高い
- **far** 副①遠くに, はるかに, 離れて ②《比較級を強めて》ずっと, はるかに 形遠い, 向こうの as far as ~と同じくらい遠く, ~まで, ~する限り(では) as far as one can できるだけ far away 遠く離れて far into ずっと far too あまりにも~過ぎる from far away 遠くから go far 遠くへ行く so far 今までのところ, これまでは
- **farm** 名農場, 農家
- **fast** 形①(速度が)速い ②(時計が)進んでいる ③しっかりした 副①速く, 急いで ②(時計が)進んで ③しっかりと, ぐっすりと stuck fast 貼り付く, 挟まって身動きが取れない
- **fat** 形太った
- **father** 名父親
- **fatten** 動太らせる, 太る, 肥やす, 肥える fatten up 太らせる
- **favorite** 形お気に入りの, ひいきの
- **fear** 名①恐れ ②心配, 不安
- **fearful** 形①恐ろしい ②心配な, 気づかって
- **fearfully** 副こわがって, こわごわ
- **fearlessly** 副恐れずに, 大胆に
- **feed** 動食物を与える
- **feel** 動感じる, (~と)思う feel like ~がほしい, ~したい気がする, ~のような感じがする feel sorry for ~をかわいそうに思う
- **feeling** 動 feel (感じる)の現在分詞 名①感じ, 気持ち ②触感, 知覚 ③同情, 思いやり, 感受性
- **feet** 名 foot (足)の複数
- **fell** 動 fall (落ちる)の過去
- **fellow** 名①仲間, 同僚 ②人, やつ
- **felt** 動 feel (感じる)の過去, 過去分詞
- **few** 形①ほとんどない, 少数の(~しかない) ②《a -》少数の, 少しはある
- **field** 名野原
- **fight** 名戦い, 争い
- **fill** 動①満ちる, 満たす ②《be -ed with ~》~でいっぱいである
- **finally** 副最後に, ついに, 結局
- **find** 動①見つける ②(~と)わかる, 気づく, ~と考える ③得る find one's way たどり着く find out 見つけ出す, 気がつく, 知る, 調べる, 解明する
- **fine** 形①元気な ②美しい, りっぱな, 申し分ない, 結構な ③晴れた ④細かい, 微妙な
- **finger** 名(手の)指 lay a finger on ~に手をかける

123

THE BEST OF GRIMM'S FAIRY TALES

- **finish** 動終わる, 終える
- **fire** 名①火, 炎, 火事 ②砲火, 攻撃 動発射する
- **first** 名最初, 第一(の人・物) 形①第一の, 最初の ②最も重要な **for the first time** 初めて **for the first time in one's life** 生まれて初めて 副第一に, 最初に
- **fish** 名魚 動釣りをする
- **fisherman** 名漁師, (趣味の)釣り人
- **flew** 動fly(飛ぶ)の過去
- **floor** 名床
- **flower** 名花, 草花
- **flute** 名フルート《楽器》
- **fly** 動飛ぶ, 飛ばす
- **folk** 名①(生活様式を共にする)人々 ②《one's -s》家族, 親類
- **follow** 動①ついていく, あとをたどる ②(〜の)結果として起こる ③(忠告などに)従う ④理解できる
- **food** 名食物, えさ, 肥料
- **food shortage** 食糧不足, 食糧難
- **fool** 名ばか者, おろかな人 動ばかにする, だます, ふざける
- **foolish** 形おろかな, ばかばかしい
- **foot** 名足
- **for** 前①《目的・原因・対象》〜にとって, 〜のために[の], 〜に対して ②《期間》〜間 ③《代理》〜の代わりに ④《方向》〜へ(向かって) **for a moment** 少しの間, 少しの間 **for a while** しばらくの間, 少しの間 **for some time** しばらくの間 **for the first time** 初めて **for the first time in one's life** 生まれて初めて **for the rest of life** 死ぬまで **for years** 何年も **for 〜 years** 〜年間, 〜年にわたって 接というわけは〜, なぜなら〜, だから
- **force** 名力, 勢い 動①強制する, 力ずくで〜する, 余儀なく〜させる ②押しやる, 押し込む
- **forest** 名森林
- **forever** 副永遠に, 絶えず

- **forget** 動忘れる, 置き忘れる
- **forgot** 動forget(忘れる)の過去, 過去分詞
- **form** 名形
- **found** 動find(見つける)の過去, 過去分詞
- **four** 名4(の数字), 4人[個] 形4の, 4人[個]の
- **fourth** 第4番目(の人・物), 4日 形第4番目の
- **free** 形①自由な, 開放された, 自由に〜できる ②暇で, (物が)空いている, 使える ③無料の **get free** 自由(の身)になる **set free** (人)を解放する, 釈放される, 自由の身になる 副①自由に ②無料で 動自由にする, 解放する
- **freshly** 副新しく, 〜したてで, 新鮮に, はつらつと
- **friend** 名友だち, 仲間
- **fright** 名恐怖, 激しい驚き
- **frightened** 形おびえた, びっくりした
- **frog** 名カエル(蛙)
- **from** 前①《出身・出発点・時間・順序・原料》〜から ②《原因・理由》〜がもとで **from far away** 遠くから **from side to side** 左右に **from then on** それ以来 **from 〜 to …** 〜から…まで
- **front** 名正面, 前 **in front of 〜**の前に, 〜の正面に
- **fruit** 名果実, 実
- **fulfill** 動(義務・約束を)果たす, (要求・条件を)満たす
- **full** 形①満ちた, いっぱいの, 満期の ②完全な, 盛りの, 充実した 名全部 **be full of** 〜で一杯である **full of holes** 穴だらけの
- **further** 副いっそう遠く, その上に, もっと

124

Word List

G

- **game** 名 ゲーム, 試合, 遊び, 競技
- **garden** 名 庭, 庭園
- **gather** 動 ①集まる, 集める ②生じる, 増す ③推測する
- **gave** 動 give（与える）の過去
- **generally** 副 ①一般に, だいたい ②たいてい
- **gently** 副 親切に, 上品に, そっと, 優しく
- **get** 動 ①得る, 手に入れる ②(ある状態に)なる, いたる ③わかる, 理解する ④〜させる, 〜を(…の状態に)する ⑤(ある場所に)達する, 着く **get angry** 腹を立てる **get away from** 〜から離れる **get back** 戻る, 帰る **get better**（病気などが）良くなる **get close to** 〜に近づく, 接近する **get down** 降りる, 着地する, 身をかがめる, ひざまずく **get free** 自由(の身)になる **get home** 家に着く[帰る] **get in** 中に入る, 乗り込む **get in or out** 出入りする **get into** 〜に入る, 入り込む, 〜に巻き込まれる **get into bed** ベッドに入る **get offered** 申し出を受ける **get out** ①外に出る, 出て行く, 逃げ出す ②取り出す, 抜き出す **get ready** 用意[支度]をする **get rid of** 〜を取り除く **get smaller** 小さくなる **get someone to do**（人）に〜させる[してもらう] **get stuck in** 〜にはまり込む **get the best of** 〜を負かす, 出し抜く **get through** 乗り切る, 〜を通り抜ける **get tired of** 〜に飽きる, 〜が嫌になる **get to**（事）を始める, 〜に達する[到着する] **get to do** 〜できるようになる, 〜できる機会を得る **get up** 起き上がる, 立ち上がる **get used to** 〜になじむ, 〜に慣れる **get 〜 back** 〜を取り戻す[戻す]
- **giant** 名 巨人, 大男
- **girl** 名 女の子, 少女
- **give** 動 ①与える, 贈る ②伝える, 述べる ③(〜を)する **give in** 降参する, 屈する,（書類などを）提出する
- **given** 動 give（与える）の過去分詞
- **glad** 形 ①うれしい, 喜ばしい ② 《be - to 〜》〜してうれしい, 喜んで〜する
- **glass** 名 ガラス(状のもの), コップ, グラス
- **go** 動 ①行く, 出かける ②動く ③進む, 経過する, いたる ④(ある状態に)なる **be going to** 〜するつもりである **go ahead** 先に行く,《許可を表す》どうぞ **go along** 〜に沿って行く,（人）について行く **go and** 〜しに行く **go back to** 〜に帰る[戻る], 〜に遡る,（中断していた作業に）再び取り掛かる **go by** ①(時が)過ぎる, 経過する ②〜のそばを通る ③〜に基づいて[よって]行う **go down** 下に降りる **go far** 遠くへ行く **go home** 帰宅する **go in** 中に入る, 開始する **go into** 〜に入る,（仕事）に就く **go off** 出かける, 去る, 出発する **go on** 続く, 続ける, 進み続ける, 起こる, 発生する **go on one's way** 道を進む, 立ち去る **go on to** 〜に移る **go out** 外出する, 外へ出る **go over to** 〜の前に[へ]行く, 〜に出向いて行く **go through** 通り抜ける, 一つずつ順番に検討する **go to bed** 床につく, 寝る **go to sleep** 寝る **go up** ①〜に上がる, 登る ②〜に近づく, 出かける **go up to** 〜まで行く, 近づく **go with** 〜と一緒に行く, 〜と調和する, 〜にとても似合う **go wrong** 失敗する, 道を踏みはずす, 調子が悪くなる **let go** 手を放す, 行かせる **off he went** 彼は出掛けた **ready to go** すっかり準備が整った
- **God** 名 神
- **gold** 名 金, 金貨, 金製品, 金色 形 金の, 金製の, 金色の
- **golden** 形 ①金色の ②金製の ③貴重な
- **gone** 動 go（行く）の過去分詞 形 去った, 使い果たした, 死んだ
- **good** 形 ①よい, 上手な, 優れた, 美しい ②(数量・程度が)かなりの, 相当な **be good at** 〜が得意である **do 〜 a good turn** 〜を助ける **good day** こんにちは **good drink** 旨い酒 **wish someone good day** （人）の一

125

The Best of Grimm's Fairy Tales

日の幸運を祈る 名《-s》①商品,品物 ②財産,所有物
- **good-bye** 名 別れのあいさつ
- **Goodness me!** 間 えっ!,おや!
- **goods** 名 ①商品,品物 ②財産,所有物
- **goose** 名 ガチョウ
- **got** 動 get(得る)の過去,過去分詞
- **government** 名 政治,政府,支配
- **grab** 動 ふいにつかむ,ひったくる
- **gray-haired** 形 白髪まじりの
- **great** 形 ①大きい,広大な,(量や程度が)たいへんな ②偉大な,優れた ③すばらしい,おもしろい
- **Gretel** 名 グレーテル《人名》
- **grew** 動 grow(成長する)の過去
- **ground** 名 地面,土,土地 fall to the ground 転ぶ on the ground 地面に
- **group** 名 集団,群
- **grow** 動 ①成長する,育つ,育てる ②増大する,大きくなる,(次第に~に)なる grow -er and -er ~にますます~する grow to ~するようになる
- **grown** 動 grow(成長する)の過去分詞
- **guard** 動 番をする,監視する,守る
- **gun** 名 銃,大砲

H

- **ha** 間 ほう,まあ,おや《驚き・悲しみ・不満・喜び・笑い声などを表す》
- **had** 動 have(持つ)の過去,過去分詞 助 have の過去《過去完了の文をつくる》 had better ~したほうが身のためだ,~しなさい
- **half** 半分 形 半分の,不完全な 副 半分,なかば,不十分に
- **hall** 名 公会堂,ホール,大広間,玄関
- **hand** 名 ①手 ②(時計の)針 ③援助の手,助け 動 手渡す hand in 差し出す,提出する hand over 手渡す,引き渡す,譲渡する
- **hang** 動 かかる,かける,つるす,ぶら下がる
- **Hansel** 名 ヘンゼル《人名》
- **happen** 動 ①(出来事が)起こる,生じる ②偶然[たまたま]~する happen to たまたま~する,偶然~する happen to be 偶然にも
- **happily** 副 幸福に,楽しく,うまく,幸いにも
- **happiness** 名 幸せ,喜び
- **happy** 形 幸せな,うれしい,幸運な,満足して be happy to do ~してうれしい,喜んで~する
- **hard** 形 ①堅い ②激しい,むずかしい ③熱心な,勤勉な ④無情な,耐えがたい,厳しい,きつい hard to ~し難い 副 ①一生懸命に ②激しく ③堅く
- **hardly** 副 ①ほとんど~でない,わずかに ②厳しく,かろうじて can hardly とても~できない
- **has** 動 have(持つ)の3人称単数現在 助 have の3人称単数現在《現在完了の文をつくる》
- **have** 動 ①持つ,持っている,抱く ②(~が)ある,いる ③食べる,飲む ④経験する,(病気に)かかる ⑤催す,開く ⑥(人に)~させる have to ~しなければならない 助《〈have + 過去分詞〉の形で現在完了の文をつくる》~した,~したことがある,ずっと~している could have done ~だったかもしれない《仮定法》 have around (人)をそばに置いておく have been to ~へ行ったことがある have no sense 理性を欠く have nothing to do with ~と何の関係もない should have done ~すべきだった(のにしなかった)《仮定法》 should never have done ~すべきではなかった(のにしてしまった)《仮定法》 will have done ~してしまっているだろう《未来進行形》

Word List

- **he** 代 彼は[が]
- **head** 名 頭 **head of the bead** ベッドの頭の方
- **heal** 動 いえる, いやす, 治る, 治す
- **healthy** 形 健康な, 健全な, 健康によい
- **hear** 動 聞く, 聞こえる **hear of ~** について聞く
- **heard** 動 hear（聞く）の過去, 過去分詞
- **heart** 名 ①心臓, 胸 ②心, 感情, ハート
- **heaven** 名 ①天国 ②天国のようなところ[状態], 楽園
- **heavily** 副 ①重く, 重そうに, ひどく ②多量に
- **heavy** 形 重い, 激しい, つらい
- **hedge** 名 生け垣, 垣根
- **held** 動 hold（つかむ）の過去, 過去分詞
- **help** 動 助ける, 手伝う
- **helpless** 形 無力の, 自分ではどうすることもできない
- **Henry** 名 ヘンリー《名》
- **her** 代 ①彼女を[に] ②彼女の
- **here** 副 ①ここに[で] ②《-is [are] ~》ここに~がある ③さあ, そら **here and there** あちこちで **here is ~** こちらは~です。 **over here** こっちへ[に]；ほら, さあ《人の注意を引く》
- **herself** 代 彼女自身
- **high** 形 ①高い ②気高い, 高価な 副 ①高く ②ぜいたくに
- **him** 代 彼を[に]
- **himself** 代 彼自身
- **his** 代 ①彼の ②彼のもの
- **hit** 動 ①打つ, なぐる ②ぶつける, ぶつかる ③命中する ④（天災などが）襲う, 打撃を与える ⑤hitの過去, 過去分詞 **hit at ~**に当てる **hit on** ふと思いつく 名 ①打撃 ②命中
- **hold** 動 ①つかむ, 持つ, 抱く ②保つ, 持ちこたえる ③収納できる, 入れることができる ④（会などを）開く **hold on** しっかりつかまる **hold up to the light** 光にかざす 名 ①つかむこと, 保有 ②支配[理解]力 **catch hold of** ~をつかむ, 捕らえる **take hold of** ~をつかむ, 捕らえる, 制する
- **hole** 名 穴 **full of holes** 穴だらけの
- **home** 名 ①家, 自国, 故郷, 家庭 ②収容所 **home** 家に着く[帰る] **go home** 帰宅する **take someone home** (人)を家まで送る 副 家に, 自国へ
- **honor** 名 名誉, 光栄 動 尊敬する, 栄誉を与える
- **horn** 名 （牛・羊などの）角, 角材
- **horse** 名 馬
- **hot** 形 暑い, 熱い
- **hour** 名 1時間, 時間
- **house** 名 家
- **how** 副 ①どうやって, どれくらい, どんなふうに ②なんて（~だろう）③《関係副詞》~する方法 **how come** どうして, なぜ **How could ~?** 何だって~なんてことがありえようか？ **how to** ~する方法 **no matter how** どんなに~であろうとも
- **however** 副 たとえ~でも 接 けれども, だが
- **human** 形 人間の, 人の 名 人間
- **hundred** 名 ①100（の数字）, 100人[個] ②《-s》何百, 多数 **hundreds of** 何百もの~ 形 ①100の, 100人[個]の ②多数の
- **hunger** 名 ①空腹, 飢え ②（~への）欲
- **hungry** 形 ①空腹の, 飢えた ②渇望して ③不毛の
- **hunt** 動 狩る, 狩りをする, 探し求める 名 狩り, 追跡
- **hunter** 名 ①狩りをする人, 狩人, ハンター ②猟馬, 猟犬
- **huntsman** 名 猟師

THE BEST OF GRIMM'S FAIRY TALES

- **huntsmen** 名 huntsman（猟師）の複数
- **hurry** 名急ぐこと, 急ぐ必要 **in a hurry** 急いで, あわてて
- **hurt** 動傷つける, 痛む, 害する 名傷, けが, 苦痛, 害
- **husband** 名夫

I

- **I** 代私は［が］
- **idea** 名考え, 意見, アイデア, 計画
- **if** 接もし～ならば, たとえ～でも, ～かどうか **as if** あたかも～のように, まるで～みたいに **ask ～ if** ～かどうか尋ねる **even if** たとえ～でも **If +《主語》+ could** ～できればなあ《仮定法》 **see if** ～かどうかを確かめる
- **ignore** 動無視する, 怠る
- **illness** 名病気
- **immediately** 副すぐに, ～するやいなや
- **important** 形重要な, 大切な, 有力な
- **in** 前①《場所・位置・所属》～（の中）に［で・の］ ②《時》～（の時）に［の・で］, ～後（に）, ～の間（に） ③《方法・手段》～で ④～を身につけて, ～を着て ⑤～に関して, ～について ⑥《状態》～の状態で 副中へ［に］, 内へ［に］
- **indeed** 副①実際, 本当に ②《強意》まったく
- **inside** 名内部［内側］に 前～の内部［内側］に
- **instead** 副その代わりに **instead of** ～の代わりに, ～をしないで
- **interesting** 形おもしろい, 興味を起こさせる
- **into** 前①《動作・運動の方向》～の中へ［に］ ②《変化》～に［へ］
- **iron** 名①鉄, 鉄製のもの ②アイロン 形鉄の, 鉄製の
- **is** 動 be（～である）の3人称単数現在
- **it** 代①それは［が］, それを［に］ ②《天候・日時・距離・寒暖などを示す》
- **its** 代それの, あれの

J

- **job** 名仕事, 職, 雇用
- **journey** 名①（遠い目的地への）旅 ②行程
- **joy** 名喜び, 楽しみ
- **jump** 動①跳ぶ, 跳躍する, 飛び越える, 飛びかかる ②（～を）熱心にやり始める **jump out of** ～から飛び出す **jump over** ～の上を飛び越える **jump up** 素早く立ち上がる **jump up and down** 飛び跳ねる
- **just** 副①まさに, ちょうど, (～した) ばかり ②ほんの, 単に, ただ～だけ ③ちょっと **just then** そのとたんに

K

- **keep** 動①とっておく, 保つ, 続ける ②（～を…に）しておく ③飼う, 養う ④経営する ⑤守る **keep one's promise** 約束を守る **keep out**（場所に）入らせない, 締め出す, ～を外に出したままにする
- **kept** 動 keep（とっておく）の過去, 過去分詞
- **kill** 動殺す, 消す, 枯らす
- **kind** 形親切な, 優しい **be kind to** ～に親切である **all kinds of** さまざまな, あらゆる種類の
- **kindly** 副親切に, 優しく
- **king** 名王, 国王
- **kingdom** 名王国
- **kiss** 名キス 動キスする
- **kitchen** 名台所, 調理場
- **knee** 名ひざ

Word List

- **knew** 動 know（知っている）の過去
- **knock** 動 ノックする, たたく, ぶつける knock over 張り倒す 名 打つこと, 戸をたたくこと［音］
- **know** 動 ①知っている, 知る,（〜が）わかる, 理解している ②知り合いである know nothing of 〜のことを知らない know of 〜について知っている
- **known** 動 know（知っている）の過去分詞 make it known that 〜を知らせる

L

- **ladies-in-waiting** 名 侍女
- **lady** 名 婦人, 夫人, 淑女, 奥さん
- **laid** 動 lay（置く）の過去, 過去分詞
- **lake** 名 湖, 湖水, 池
- **land** 名 ①陸地, 土地 ②国, 領域 動 上陸する, 着地する
- **landlord** 名（男の）家主, 地主
- **language** 名 言語, 言葉, 国語, 〜語, 専門語
- **large** 形 ①大きい, 広い ②大勢の, 多量の
- **last** 形 ①《the -》最後の ②この前の, 先〜 ③最新の 副 ①最後に ②この前 at last ついに, とうとう 名《the -》最後（のもの）, 終わり 動 続く, 持ちこたえる
- **late** 形 ①遅い, 後期の ②最近の 副 ①遅れて, 遅く ②最近まで, 以前
- **later** 副 後で, 後ほど
- **latest** 形 ①最新の, 最近の ②最も遅い
- **laugh** 動 笑う make someone laugh（人）を笑わせる
- **lay** 動 ①置く, 横たえる, 敷く ②整える ③卵を産む ④lie（横たわる）の過去 lay a finger on 〜に手をかける

- **lead** 動 ①導く, 案内する ②（生活を）送る lead into（ある場所）へ行く lead to 〜に至る, 〜に通じる, 〜を引き起こす
- **learn** 動 学ぶ, 習う, 教わる, 知識［経験］を得る
- **least** 名 最小, 最少 at least 少なくとも
- **leave** 動 ①出発する, 去る ②残す, 置き忘れる ③（〜を…の）ままにしておく ④ゆだねる leave 〜 alone 〜をそっとしておく leave 〜 for … …を〜のために残しておく
- **led** 動 lead（導く）の過去, 過去分詞
- **left** 形 左の, 左側の 動 leave（去る, 〜をあとに残す）の過去, 過去分詞
- **leg** 名 ①脚, すね ②支柱
- **less** 形 〜より小さい［少ない］ 副 〜より少なく, 〜ほどでなく
- **let** 動（人に〜）させる,（〜するのを）許す,（〜をある状態に）する let be そのままにしておく let go 手を放す, 行かせる let in 〜を招き入れる
- **lie** 動 ①うそをつく ②横たわる, 寝る ③（ある状態に）ある, 存在する lie dead 死んで横たわっている lie down 横たわる, 横になる
- **life** 名 ①生命, 生物 ②一生, 生涯, 人生 ③生活, 暮らし, 世の中 all one's life ずっと, 生まれてから for the first time in one's life 生まれて初めて for the rest of life 死ぬまで
- **lift** 動 持ち上げる, 上がる
- **light** 名 光, 明かり hold up to the light 光にかざす 動 火をつける, 照らす, 明るくする
- **like** 動 好む, 好きである would like to 〜したいと思う 前 〜に似ている, 〜のような feel like 〜がほしい, 〜したい気がする, 〜のような感じがする like this このような, こんなふうに look like 〜のように見える, 〜に似ている 形 似ている, 〜のような 接 あたかも〜のように 名 ①好きなもの ②《the [one's] -》同じ

THE BEST OF GRIMM'S FAIRY TALES

ようなもの[人]

- **likely** 形 ①ありそうな, (〜)しそうな ②適当な 副たぶん, おそらく
- **line** 名線, 糸
- **listen** 動《— to 〜》〜を聞く, 〜に耳を傾ける
- **little** 形 ①小さい, 幼い ②少しの, 短い ③ほとんど〜ない, 《a —》少しはある **a little way** 少し
- **live** 動住む, 暮らす, 生きている **there lived 〜.** 〜が住んでいました。
- **lively** 形 ①元気のよい, 活発な ②鮮やかな, 強烈な, 真に迫った
- **lives** 名 life(生命)の複数
- **long** 形 ①長い, 長期の ②《長さ・距離・時間などを示す語句を伴って》〜の長さ[距離・時間]の **long way** はるかに 副長い間, ずっと **all day long** 一日中, 終日 やがて, まもなく **no longer** もはや〜でない[〜しない] **not 〜 any longer** もはや〜でない[〜しない] 名長い期間 動切望する, 思い焦がれる
- **look** 動 ①見る ②(〜に)見える, (〜の)顔つきをする ③注意する ④《間投詞のように》ほら, ねえ **look after** 〜の世話をする, 〜に気をつける **look around** まわりを見回す **look back at** 〜に視線を戻す, 〜を振り返って見る **look down** 見下ろす **look down at** 〜に目[視線]を落とす **look down upon** 見下す, 俯瞰する **look for** 〜を探す **look like** 〜のように見える, 〜に似ている **look up** 見上げる, 調べる
- **loosen** 動 ①ゆるめる, ほどく ②解き放つ
- **lord** 名首長, 主人, 領主, 貴族, 上院議員
- **lose** 動 ①失う, 迷う, 忘れる ②負ける, 失敗する
- **lost** 動 lose(失う)の過去, 過去分詞
- **lot** 名 ①くじ, 運 ②地所, 区画 ③たくさん, たいへん, 《a — of 〜 /-s of 〜》たくさんの〜 ④やつ, 連中

- **loud** 形大声の, 騒がしい
- **loudly** 副大声で, 騒がしく
- **love** 名愛, 愛情, 思いやり 動愛する, 恋する, 大好きである
- **lovely** 形愛らしい, 美しい, すばらしい
- **low** 形 ①低い, 弱い ②低級の, 劣等な
- **luck** 名運, 幸運, めぐり合わせ
- **lunch** 名昼食, ランチ, 軽食
- **lying** 動 lie(横たわる)の現在分詞

M

- **mad** 形 ①気の狂った ②逆上した, 理性をなくした ③ばかげた ④(〜に)熱中[熱中]して, 夢中の
- **made** 動 make(作る)の過去, 過去分詞 形作った, 作られた **be made of** 〜でできて[作られて]いる
- **madman** 名 ①狂人 ②常軌を逸した人
- **magic** 名 ①魔法, 手品 ②魔力 形魔法の, 魔力のある
- **main** 形主な, 主要な
- **make** 動 ①作る, 得る ②行う ③(〜に)なる ③(〜を…に)する, (〜を…)させる **make a bad stroke** (おのを)ドろし損ねる **make an end of** 〜をおしまいにする **make everything right** 全てうまくいかせる **make it known that** 〜を知らせる **make someone laugh** (人)を笑わせる **make straight for** 〜に直行する **make sure** 確かめる, 確認する **make up** 作り出す, 考え出す, 〜を構成[形成]する **make up one's mind** 決心する
- **man** 名男性, 人, 人類
- **many** 形多数の, たくさんの
- **mark** 名印, 記号, 跡
- **market** 名市場, マーケット
- **marriage** 名結婚(生活・式)

WORD LIST

- **married** 動 marry（結婚する）の過去, 過去分詞 形結婚した, 既婚の
- **marry** 動結婚する **marry off** 嫁がせる
- **master** 名主人, 雇い主, 師, 名匠
- **match** 名①試合, 勝負 ②相手, 釣り合うもの
- **material** 名材料, 原料
- **matter** 名物, 事, 事件, 問題 **no matter how** どんなに〜であろうとも 動《主に疑問文・否定文で》重要である
- **may** 助①〜かもしれない ②〜してもよい, 〜できる **May I 〜?** 〜してもよいですか。
- **maybe** 副たぶん, おそらく
- **me** 代私を[に]
- **meal** 名食事
- **meant** 動 mean（意味する）の過去, 過去分詞
- **measure** 動①測る, (〜の)寸法がある ②評価する
- **member** 名一員, メンバー
- **men** 名 man（男性）の複数
- **met** 動 meet（会う）の過去, 過去分詞
- **middle** 名中間, 最中 **in the middle of** 〜の真ん中[中ほど]に
- **might** 助《mayの過去》①〜かもしれない ②〜してもよい, 〜できる
- **mighty** 形強力な, 権勢のある
- **mile** 名マイル《長さの単位。1,609m》
- **milk** 名牛乳, ミルク
- **mind** 名①心, 精神, 考え ②知性 **make up one's mind** 決心する 動①気にする, いやがる ②気をつける, 用心する **Never mind.** 気にするな。
- **mine** 代私のもの
- **minute** 名①（時間の）分 ②ちょっとの間 **in a minute** すぐに **this minute** 今すぐ

- **miss** 動失敗する, 免れる, 〜を見逃す, (目標を)はずす
- **moment** 名①瞬間, ちょっとの間 ②(特定の)時, 時期 **for a moment** 少しの間
- **money** 名金, 通貨 **save money** コストを削減する, 貯金する
- **month** 名月, 1カ月
- **moon** 名月, 月光
- **more** 形①もっと多くの ②それ以上の, 余分の **no more** もう〜ない 副もっと, さらに多く, いっそう **more than** 〜以上 名もっと多くの物[人] **not 〜 any more** もう[これ以上]〜ない **once more** もう一度
- **morning** 名朝, 午前
- **most** 形①最も多い ②たいていの, 大部分の 副最も(多く) **most welcome** 大歓迎
- **mother** 名母, 母親
- **mountain** 名①山《the 〜 M-s》山脈 ③山のようなもの, 多量
- **mouth** 名①口 ②言葉, 発言
- **move** 動①動く, 動かす ②感動させる ③引っ越す, 移動する **move away** ①立ち去る ②移す, 動かす
- **much** 形(量・程度が)多くの, 多量の 副①とても, たいへん ②《比較級・最上級を修飾して》ずっと, はるかに **too much** 過度の
- **music** 名音楽, 楽曲
- **must** 助①〜しなければならない ②〜に違いない
- **my** 代私の
- **myself** 代私自身

N

- **nail** 名くぎ, びょう
- **near** 前〜の近くに, 〜のそばに 副近くに, 親密で
- **nearby** 形近くの, 間近の

- **nearly** 副 ①近くに, 親しく ②ほとんど, あやうく
- **neck** 名 首, (衣服の)えり
- **need** 動 (~を)必要とする, 必要である **need to do** ~する必要がある 助 ~する必要がある
- **neighbor** 名 隣人, 隣り合うもの
- **never** 決して[少しも]~ない, 一度も[二度と]~ない **Never mind.** 気にするな。
- **nevertheless** 副 それにもかかわらず, それでもやはり
- **new** 形 ①新しい, 新規の ②新鮮な, できたての
- **next** 形 ①次の, 翌~ ②隣の **next to** ~のとなりに, ~の次に 副 ①次に ②隣に 代 次の人[もの]
- **nice** 形 すてきな, よい, きれいな, 親切な
- **night** 名 夜, 晩 **the night before** 前の晩
- **no** 副 ①いいえ, いや ②少しも~ない **no longer** もはや~でない[~しない] **no matter how** どんなに~であろうとも **no more** もう~ない **no sooner** ~するや否や **no use** 役に立たない, 用をなさない 形 ~がない, 少しも~ない, ~どころでない, ~禁止 名 否定, 拒否
- **no one** 誰も[一人も]~ない
- **nobody** 代 誰も[1人も]~ない
- **noise** 名 騒音, 騒ぎ, 物音
- **not** 副 ~でない, ~しない **not at all** 少しも~でない **not ~ but (also)** …~だけでなく…もまた **not ~ any longer** もはや~でない[~しない] **not ~ any more** もう[これ以上]~ない **not ~ at all** 少しも[全然]~ない **not ~ but** …~ではなくて…
- **nothing** 代 何も~ない[しない] **have nothing to do with** ~と何の関係もない **know nothing of** ~のことを知らない
- **notice** 動 ①気づく, 認める ②通告する
- **now** 副 ①今(では), 現在 ②今すぐに ③では, さて ④たった今 **right now** 今すぐに 形 今の, 現在の
- **number** 名 ①数, 数字, 番号 ②~号, ~番 ③《-s》多数

O

- **o'clock** 副 ~時
- **object** 動 反対する, 異議を唱える
- **objectionable** 形 反対すべき, 好ましくない, 不愉快な
- **ocean** 名 海, 大洋,《the ~ O-》~洋
- **of** 前 ①《所有・所属・部分》~の, ~に属する ②《性質・特徴・材料》~の, ~製の ③《部分》~のうち ④《分離・除去》~から
- **off** 副 ①離れて ②はずれて ③止まって ④休んで **be off to** ~へ出かける **off with** (すばやく)~を取り去る **take the rest of the day off** 今日はもう帰る 形 ①離れて ②季節はずれの ③休みの 前 ~を離れて, ~をはずれて, (値段が)~引きの
- **offer** 動 申し出る, 申し込む, 提供する **get offered** 申し出を受ける 名 提案, 提供
- **often** 副 しばしば, たびたび
- **oh** 間 ああ, おや, まあ
- **okay** 形 《許可, 同意, 満足などを表して》よろしい, 正しい
- **old** 形 ①年取った, 老いた ②~歳の ③古い, 昔の
- **old folks** 老人たち
- **on** 前 ①《場所・接触》~(の上)に ②《日・時》~に, ~と同時に, ~のすぐ後に ③《関係・従事》~に関して, ~について, ~して 副 ①身につけて, 上に ②前へ, 続けて **on and on** 延々と, 長々と, 引き続き
- **once** 副 ①一度, 1回 ②かつて **once more** もう一度 **once upon a**

Word List

- **time** むかしむかし 名一度, 1回 **at once** すぐに, 同時に
- **Once upon a time** むかしむかしある時《おとぎ話の始めの決まり文句》
- **one** 名 1 (の数字), 1人[個] 形 ①1の, 1人[個]の ②ある~ ③《the -》唯一の **one day** (過去の)ある日, (未来の)いつか 代 ①(一般の)人, ある物 ②一方, 片方 ③~なもの **one of** ~の1つ[人] **one side** 片側 **this one** これ, こちら
- **only** 形唯一の 副 ①単に, ~にすぎない, ただ~だけ ②やっと **not only ~ but (also)** … ~だけでなく…もまた
- **onto** 前~の上へ[に]
- **open** 形 ①開いた, 広々とした ②公開された 動 ①開く, 始まる ②広がる, 広げる ③打ち明ける **open up** 広がる, 広げる, 開く, 開ける
- **opening** 名開いた所, 穴
- **or** 接 ①~か…, または ②さもないと ③すなわち, 言い換えると
- **order** 動 ①(~するよう)命じる, 注文する ②整頓する, 整理する
- **other** 形 ①ほかの, 異なった ②(2つのうち)もう一方の, (3つ以上のうち)残りの **on the other side of ~** の反対側に 代 ①ほかの人[物] ②《the -》残りの1つ
- **our** 代私たちの
- **ourselves** 代私たち自身
- **out** 副 ①外へ[に], 不在で, 離れて ②世に出て ③消えて ④すっかり **out of** ~から外へ, ~から抜け出して ②~から作り出して, ~を材料として ③~の範囲外に, ~から離れて ④(ある数)の中から **out of breath** 息を切らして **out of sight** 見えないところに **out of the wood** 森の中から出て 形 ①外に, 遠く離れた ②公表された 前 ~から外へ[に] 動 ①追い出す ②露見する ③(スポーツで)アウトにする
- **outside** 形外部の, 外側の 副外へ, 外側に 前~の外に[で・の・へ], ~の範囲を越えて
- **over** 前 ①~の上の[に], ~を一面に覆って ②~を越えて, ~以上に, ~よりまさって ③~の向こう側の[に] ④~の間 副上に, 一面に, ずっと **over here** こっちへ[に]; ほら, さあ《人の注意を引く》 **over there** あそこに
- **overcame** 動 overcome (勝つ)の過去
- **own** 形自身の
- **owner** 名持ち主, オーナー

P

- **pain** 名痛み, 苦悩
- **painting** 名絵画, 油絵
- **pair** 名 (2つから成る)一対, 一組, ペア 動対になる[する]
- **palace** 名宮殿, 大邸宅
- **parent** 名《-s》両親
- **part** 名 ①部分, 割合 ②役目 動分ける, 分かれる, 別れる **part with ~** を手放す
- **pass** 動 ①過ぎる, 通る ②(年月が)たつ ③(試験に)合格する ④手渡す **pass by** ~のそばを通る[通り過ぎる]
- **past** 前《時間・場所》~を過ぎて, ~を越して 副通り越して, 過ぎて
- **path** 名 ①(踏まれてきた)小道, 歩道 ②進路, 通路
- **pay** 動支払う, 払う, 報いる 名給料, 報い
- **peacefully** 副平和に, 穏やかに
- **people** 名 ①(一般に)人々 ②民衆, 世界の人々, 国民, 民族 ③人間
- **perhaps** 副たぶん, ことによると
- **pick** 動 ①(花・果実などを)摘む, もぐ ②選ぶ, 精選する ③つつく, ついて穴をあける, ほじくり出す ④(~を)摘み取る **pick off** ~をもぎとる **pick out** 拾い出す, えり抜く, 選

The Best of Grimm's Fairy Tales

び出す pick up 拾い上げる

- ☐ **piece** 名 ①一片, 部分 ②1個, 1本
- ☐ **place** 名 ①場所, 建物 ②余地, 空間 ③《one's -》家, 部屋 in place of ～の代わりに take place 行われる, 起こる
- ☐ **plan** 名 計画, 設計(図), 案
- ☐ **plant** 名 植物, 草木
- ☐ **plate** 名 (浅い)皿, 1皿の料理
- ☐ **play** 動 ①遊ぶ, 競技する ②(楽器を)演奏する, (役を)演じる child's play 非常に簡単なこと, 朝飯前のこと 名 遊び, 競技, 劇 play with ～で遊ぶ, ～と一緒に遊ぶ
- ☐ **please** 動 喜ばす, 満足させる be pleased to do ～してうれしい be pleased with ～が気に入る 間 どうぞ, お願いします
- ☐ **pleased** 形 喜んだ, 気に入った
- ☐ **pleasure** 名 喜び, 楽しみ, 満足, 娯楽
- ☐ **pocket** 名 ポケット, 袋
- ☐ **point** 名 ①先, 先端 ②点 ③地点, 時点, 箇所 ④《the -》要点
- ☐ **poor** 形 ①貧しい, 乏しい, 粗末な, 貧弱な ②劣った, へたな ③不幸な, 哀れな, 気の毒な
- ☐ **position** 名 ①位置, 場所, 姿勢 ②地位, 身分, 職 ③立場, 状況
- ☐ **possibly** 副 ①あるいは, たぶん ②《否定文, 疑問文で》どうしても, できる限り, とても, なんとか
- ☐ **pour** 動 ①注ぐ, 浴びせる ②流れ出る, 流れ込む ③ざあざあ降る
- ☐ **power** 名 力, 能力, 才能, 勢力, 権力
- ☐ **powerful** 形 力強い, 実力のある, 影響力のある
- ☐ **praise** 動 ほめる, 賞賛する
- ☐ **pray** 動 祈る, 懇願する
- ☐ **pretend** 動 ①ふりをする, 装う ②あえて～しようとする
- ☐ **pretty** 形 ①かわいい, きれいな ②相当な
- ☐ **price** 名 ①値段, 代価 ②《-s》物価, 相場
- ☐ **prince** 名 王子, プリンス
- ☐ **princess** 名 王女
- ☐ **probably** 副 たぶん, あるいは
- ☐ **problem** 名 問題, 難問
- ☐ **promise** 名 ①約束 ②有望 keep one's promise 約束を守る 動 ①約束する ②見込みがある
- ☐ **proudly** 副 ①誇らしげに ②うぬぼれて
- ☐ **prove** 動 ①証明する ②(～である ことが)わかる, (～と)なる
- ☐ **pull** 動 ①引く, 引っ張る ②引きつける pull in 引っ込める, (網, 釣り糸を)引く pull off 離れる, 去る, (衣服などを)脱ぐ pull out 引き抜く, 引き出す, 取り出す pull up 引っ張り上げる
- ☐ **push** 動 ①押す, 押し進む, 押し進める ②進む, 突き出る push back 押し返す, 押しのける push out 突き出す push someone out of (人)を～からたたき出す 名 押し, 突進, 後援
- ☐ **put** 動 ①置く, のせる ②入れる, つける ③(ある状態に)する ④putの過去, 過去分詞 put back (もとの場所に)戻す, 返す put in ～の中に入れる put off ～から逃れる, 延期する, 要求をそらす, 不快にさせる, やめさせる put on ①～を身につける, 着る ②～を…の上に置く put out 外に出す, (手など)を(差し)出す

Q

- ☐ **queen** 名 女王, 王妃
- ☐ **quick** 形 (動作が)速い, すばやい
- ☐ **quickly** 副 敏速に, 急いで
- ☐ **quietly** 副 ①静かに ②平穏に, 控えめに
- ☐ **quite** 副 ①まったく, すっかり, 完全に ②かなり, ずいぶん ③ほとんど

WORD LIST

R

- **rain** 名雨,降雨
- **ran** 動run(走る)の過去
- **rather** 副①むしろ,かえって ②かなり,いくぶん,やや ③それどころか逆に would rather ~する方がよい
- **reach** 動①着く,到着する,届く ②手を伸ばして取る
- **read** 動読む,読書する
- **ready** 形用意[準備]ができた,まさに~しようとする,今にも~せんばかりの be ready to すぐに[いつでも]・できる ~する構えで get ready 用意[支度]をする ready to go すっかり準備が整った 動用意[準備]する
- **real** 形実際の,実在する,本物の
- **realize** 動理解する,実現する
- **really** 副本当に,実際に,確かに
- **reason** 名①理由 ②理性,道理
- **receive** 動受け取る,受領する
- **red** 形赤い 名赤,赤色
- **remain** 動①残っている,残る ②(~の)ままである[いる]
- **remember** 動思い出す,覚えている,忘れないでいる
- **remove** 動取り去る,除去する
- **renew** 動新しくする,更新する,回復する,再開する
- **replace** 動①取り替える,差し替える ②元に戻す
- **reply** 動答える,返事をする,応答する
- **require** 動①必要とする,要する ②命じる,請求する
- **resign** 動辞職する,やめる,断念する
- **rest** 名①休息 ②安静 ③休止,停止 ④(the -)残り for the rest of life 死ぬまで take a rest 休息する take the rest of the day off 今日はもう帰る 動①休む,眠る ②休止する,静止する ③(~に)基づいている ④(~の)ままである
- **return** 動帰る,戻る,返す
- **rich** 形①富んだ,金持ちの ②豊かな,濃い,深い
- **rid** 動取り除く get rid of ~を取り除く
- **right** 形①正しい ②適切な ③健全な ④右(側)の make everything right 全てうまくいかせる 副①まっすぐに,すぐに ②右(側)に ③ちょうど,正確に right away すぐに right now 今すぐに,たった今
- **right-hand man** 最も頼りになる人,右腕
- **ring** 名①輪 円形,指輪
- **risen** 動rise(昇る)の過去分詞
- **road** 名①道路,道,通り ②手段,方法 winding road 曲がりくねった道
- **rode** 動ride(乗る)の過去
- **roll** 動転がる,転がす
- **roof** 名屋根(のようなもの),住居
- **room** 名①部屋 ②空間,余地 take a room (宿で)部屋を取る
- **rose** 名①バラ(の花) ②バラ色 動rise(昇る)の過去
- **round** 形①丸い,円形の ②ちょうど 副①周りに 前①~を回って ②~の周囲に 動①丸くなる[する] ②回る
- **row** 名①(横に並んだ)列 ②舟をこぐこと ③論争,騒ぎ in a row 1列に(並んで),連続して
- **ruler** 名支配者
- **run** 動①走る ②運行する ③(川が)流れる ④経営する run after ~を追いかける run away 走り去る,逃げ出す run down 流れ出す run into ~に駆け込む,~の中に走って入る run off into ~の中に逃げ込む run off 走り去る,逃げ去る run out of ~が不足する,~を使い果たす
- **rush** 動突進する,せき立てる

rush in ～に突入する, ～に駆けつける

S

- [ ] **sadly** 副悲しそうに, 不幸にも
- [ ] **sadness** 名悲しみ, 悲哀
- [ ] **safe** 形安全な, 危険のない
- [ ] **said** 動say（言う）の過去, 過去分詞
- [ ] **sail** 動帆走する, 航海する, 出航する
- [ ] **same** 形①同じ, 同様の ②前述の the same ～ as ………と同じ（ような）～ 代《the -》同一の人［物］ 副《the -》同様に
- [ ] **sang** 動sing（歌う）の過去
- [ ] **sat** 動sit（座る）の過去, 過去分詞
- [ ] **save** 動①救う, 守る ②とっておく, 節約する save money コストを削減する, 貯金する
- [ ] **saw** 動see（見る）の過去
- [ ] **say** 動言う, 口に出す say to oneself ひとり言を言う, 心に思う
- [ ] **school** 名学校
- [ ] **schooling** 名学校教育, 教室授業, スクーリング
- [ ] **sea** 名海
- [ ] **seashore** 名海岸, 海辺
- [ ] **seat** 名席, 座席, 位置 動着席させる, すえつける
- [ ] **second** 形第2の, 2番の
- [ ] **secret** 形①秘密の, 隠れた ②神秘の, 不思議な 名秘密, 神秘
- [ ] **see** 動①見る, 見える, 見物する ②（～と）わかる, 認識する, 経験する ③会う ④考える, 確かめる, 調べる ⑤気をつける see if ～かどうかを確かめる
- [ ] **seem** 動（～に）見える,（～のように）思われる seem to be ～であるように思われる
- [ ] **seen** 動see（見る）の過去分詞
- [ ] **sell** 動売る, 売っている, 売れる
- [ ] **send** 動送る send for ～を呼びにやる, ～を呼び寄せる
- [ ] **sense** 名①感覚, 感じ ②《-s》意識, 正気, 本性 ③常識, 分別, センス ④意味 have no sense 理性を欠く
- [ ] **sent** 動send（送る）の過去, 過去分詞
- [ ] **servant** 名召使, 使用人, しもべ
- [ ] **service** 名①勤務, 業務 ②奉仕, 貢献
- [ ] **set** 動①置く, 当てる, つける ②整える, 設定する ③（太陽・月などが）沈む ④（～を…の状態に）する, させる ⑤setの過去, 過去分詞 set a date 日取りを決める set free（人）を解放する, 釈放される, 自由の身になる set off 出発する, 発射する set out ①出発する, 置く ②配置する
- [ ] **settle** 動①安定する［させる］, 落ち着く, 落ち着かせる ②《- in ～》～に移り住む, 定住する settle down 落ち着く, 興奮がおさまる
- [ ] **seven** 名7（の数字）, 7人［個］ 形7の, 7人［個］の
- [ ] **several** 形①いくつかの ②めいめいの
- [ ] **shade** 名陰, 日陰
- [ ] **shall** 助①《Iが主語で》～するだろう, ～だろう ②《I以外が主語で》(～に)～させよう,（…は）～することになるだろう
- [ ] **share** 動分配する, 共有する
- [ ] **sharp** 形鋭い, とがった
- [ ] **she** 代彼女は［が］
- [ ] **shine** 動①光る, 輝く ②光らせる, 磨く
- [ ] **shiny** 形輝く, 光る
- [ ] **ship** 名船, 飛行船
- [ ] **shoe** 名《-s》靴
- [ ] **shone** 動shine（光る）の過去, 過去分詞
- [ ] **shook** 動shake（振る）の過去
- [ ] **shop** 名店, 小売店

WORD LIST

- **shore** 名岸, 海岸, 陸
- **short** 形短い
- **shortage** 名不足, 欠乏
- **shot** 名①発砲, 銃撃 ②弾丸 take a shot at ～を狙い撃ちする
- **should** 助～すべきである, ～したほうがよい should have done ～すべきだった（のにしなかった）《仮定法》 should never have done ～すべきではなかった（のにしてしまった）《仮定法》
- **shoulder** 名肩
- **shout** 動叫ぶ, 大声で言う, どなりつける
- **show** 動①表示, 見世物, ショー ②外見, 様子
- **shut** 動①閉まる, 閉める, 閉じる ②たたむ ③閉じ込める ④shutの過去, 過去分詞
- **side** 名側, 横, そば, 斜面 either side of ～の両側に from side to side 左右に on either side 両側に on the other side of ～の反対側に one side 片側 side by side 並んで
- **sight** 名①見ること, 視力, 視界 ②光景, 眺め ③見解 out of sight 見えないところに
- **silver** 名銀, 銀貨, 銀色 形銀製の
- **simple** 形①単純な, 簡単な, 質素な ②単一の, 単独の ③普通の, ただの
- **simply** 副①簡単に ②単に, ただ ③まったく, 完全に
- **sing** 動①(歌を)歌う ②さえずる
- **sister** 名①姉妹, 姉, 妹 ②修道女
- **sit** 動①座る, 腰掛ける ②止まる ③位置する sit on ～の上に乗る, ～の上に乗って動けないようにする
- **sitting** 名 at one sitting 1回で
- **six** 名6(の数字), 6人[個] 形6の, 6人[個]の
- **size** 名大きさ, 寸法, サイズ
- **skin** 名皮膚, 皮, 革(製品)
- **sky** 名①空, 天空, 大空 ②天気, 空模様, 気候
- **sleep** 動眠る, 寝る go to sleep 寝る sleep in 寝床に入る 名睡眠
- **sleeping** 形眠っている
- **slept** 動 sleep (眠る)の過去, 過去分詞
- **small** 形①小さい, 少ない ②取るに足りない get smaller 小さくなる
- **smell** 動①(～の)においがする ②においをかぐ ③かぎつける, 感づく 名①嗅覚 ②におい, 香り
- **smiling** 形笑みを浮かべている
- **snore** 名いびき
- **snow-white** 形雪のように白い
- **so** 副①とても ②同様に, ～もまた ③《先行する句・節の代用》そのように, そう as A so B A と同様に B so far 今までのところ, これまでは so that ～するために, それで, ～できるように so ～ that … 非常に～ので… 接①だから, それで ②では, さて
- **soft** 形柔らかい, 手ざわり[口あたり]のよい
- **soil** 名土, 土地
- **soldier** 名兵士, 兵卒
- **some** 形①いくつかの, 多少の ②ある, 誰か, 何か for some time しばらくの間 some time いつか, そのうち 副約, およそ 代①いくつか ②ある人[物]たち
- **somehow** 副①どうにかこうにか, ともかく, 何とかして ②どういうわけか
- **someone** 代ある人, 誰か
- **something** 代①ある物, 何か ②いくぶん, 多少 something to do 何か～すべきこと
- **sometimes** 副時々, 時たま
- **somewhere** 副①どこかへ[に] ②いつか, およそ
- **son** 名息子, 子弟, ～の子
- **son-in-law** 名娘むこ
- **song** 名歌, 詩歌, 鳴き声

- □ **soon** 副 まもなく, すぐに, すみやかに as soon as ～するとすぐに, ～するや否や no sooner ～するや否や
- □ **sorry** 形 気の毒に [申し訳なく] 思う, 残念な feel sorry for ～をかわいそうに思う
- □ **sort** 名 種類, 品質 what sort of どういう
- □ **sound** 名 音, 騒音, 響き, サウンド
- □ **soundly** 副 健全に, 堅実に, 徹底的に
- □ **spare** 形 予備の
- □ **speak** 動 話す, 言う, 演説する speak about ～について話す
- □ **special** 形 特別の, 特殊の
- □ **spend** 動 ①(金などを)使う, 消費[浪費]する ②(時を)過ごす
- □ **spin** 動 ①つむぐ ②(ガラス, 金などを)糸にする ③(カイコやクモが糸を)吐く ④ぐるぐる回る, スピンする spin into thread 糸につむぐ
- □ **spinning** 名 糸紡ぎ
- □ **spinning wheel** 糸車
- □ **spirit** 名 霊
- □ **spoke** 動 speak (話す) の過去
- □ **spring** 動 跳ねる, 跳ぶ
- □ **spun** 動 spin (紡ぐ) の過去, 過去分詞
- □ **stable** 名 馬小屋, 厩舎
- □ **stair** 名 ①(階段の)1段 ②《-s》階段, はしご
- □ **stand** 動 ①立つ, 立たせる, 立っている, ある ②耐える, 立ち向かう stand by そばに立つ stand for ～を意味する, ～を支持する, ～を我慢する, ～をこらえる stand up to ～に耐える 名 台, 屋台, スタンド
- □ **start** 動 ①出発する, 始まる, 始める ②生じる, 生じさせる start doing ～し始める start to do ～し始める
- □ **stay** 動 ①とどまる, 泊まる, 滞在する ②持続する, (～の)ままでいる stay in 家にいる, (場所)に泊まる, 滞在する stay with ～の所に泊まる
- □ **step** 名 歩み, 1歩(の距離) 動 歩む, 踏む step on ～を踏みつける step out 外へ出る
- □ **stepmother** 名 義母, 継母
- □ **stick** 名 棒, 杖 動 ①(突き)刺さる, 刺す ②くっつく, くっつける ③突き出る ④《受け身で》いきづまる stick out of ～から突き出す stick to くっつく, 張り付く
- □ **sticky** 形 くっつく, 粘着性の
- □ **still** 副 ①まだ, 今でも ②それでも(なお) 形 静止した, 静かな
- □ **stone** 名 ①石, 小石 ②宝石 形 石の, 石製の
- □ **stood** 動 stand (立つ) の過去, 過去分詞
- □ **stop** 動 ①やめる, やめさせる, 止める, 止まる ②立ち止まる stop doing ～するのをやめる stop to ～しようと立ち止まる
- □ **stopper** 名 栓, 詰め, 止め具
- □ **storm** 名 嵐, 暴風雨
- □ **story** 名 物語, 話
- □ **straight** 形 ①一直線の, まっすぐな, 直立 [垂直] の ②率直な, 整然とした make straight for ～に直行する 副 ①一直線に, まっすぐに, 垂直に ②率直に straight away すぐに
- □ **strange** 形 ①知らない, 見[聞き]慣れない ②奇妙な, 変わった
- □ **strange-looking** 形 変な様子の, 奇妙な顔つきの
- □ **strength** 名 ①力, 体力 ②長所, 強み ③強さ, 濃度
- □ **stretch** 動 引き伸ばす, 広がる, 広げる
- □ **stroke** 名 ①一撃, 一打ち ②一動作 ③一なで, 一さすり make a bad stroke (おのを)下ろし損ねる
- □ **strong** 形 強い, 堅固な, 強烈な
- □ **strongly** 副 強く, 頑丈に, 猛烈に, 熱心に
- □ **stuck** 動 stick (刺さる) の過去, 過

Word List

去分詞 **be stuck fast** 貼り付く **become stuck** (異物が)詰まる **get stuck in** ～にはまり込む **stuck fast** 貼り付く, 挟まって身動きが取れない

- [ ] **student** 名 学生, 生徒
- [ ] **study** 動 勉強する, 研究する
- [ ] **succeed** 動 成功する **succeed in doing** ～する事に成功する
- [ ] **success** 名 成功, 幸運, 上首尾
- [ ] **successful** 形 成功した, うまくいった
- [ ] **such** 形 ①そのような, このような ②そんなに, とても, 非常に **such a** そのような **such ～ that …** 非常に～なので…
- [ ] **suddenly** 副 突然, 急に
- [ ] **sugar** 名 砂糖
- [ ] **sugary** 形 砂糖の, 甘い, 甘ったるい
- [ ] **summer** 名 夏
- [ ] **sun** 名 《the -》太陽, 日
- [ ] **sunlight** 名 日光
- [ ] **suppose** 動 ①仮定する, 推測する ②《be -d to ～》～することになっている, ～するものである
- [ ] **sure** 形 確かな, 確実な.《be - to ～》必ず［きっと］～する, 確信して **make sure** 確かめる, 確認する
- [ ] **surprise** 名 驚き, 不意打ち **to one's surprise** ～が驚いたことに
- [ ] **surprised** 形 驚いた
- [ ] **swam** 動 swim (泳ぐ)の過去
- [ ] **swan** 名 ハクチョウ(白鳥)
- [ ] **sweet** 形 甘い 名 ①《-s》甘い菓子 ②甘い味［香り］, 甘いもの
- [ ] **swim** 動 泳ぐ **swim up** 泳ぎ上る
- [ ] **sword** 名 剣, 刀

T

- [ ] **table** 名 テーブル, 食卓
- [ ] **tailor** 名 仕立屋, テーラー
- [ ] **take** 動 ①取る, 持つ ②持って［連れて］いく, 捕らえる ③乗る ④(時間・労力を)費やす, 必要とする ⑤(ある動作を)する ⑥飲む ⑦耐える, 受け入れる **take a chance** いちかばちかやってみる **take a rest** 休息する **take a room** (宿で)部屋を取る **take a shot at** ～を狙い撃ちする **take care** 気をつける, 注意する **take care of** ～の世話をする, ～の面倒を見る, ～を管理する **take hold of** ～をつかむ, 捕らえる, 制する **take into** 手につかむ, 中に取り入れる **take off** (衣服を)脱ぐ, 取り去る, ～を取り除く, 離陸する, 出発する **take out** 取り出す, 取り外す, 連れ出す, 持って帰る **take out of** ～から出す, ～に連れ出す **take over** 引き継ぐ, 支配する, 乗っ取る **take place** 行われる, 起こる **take someone home** (人)を家まで送る **take the rest of the day off** 今日はもう帰る **take ～ to …** ～を…に連れて行く
- [ ] **talk** 動 話す, 語る, 相談する
- [ ] **tall** 形 高い, 背の高い
- [ ] **tap** 動 軽くポンとたたく, たたいて合図する
- [ ] **taste** 動 味がする, 味わう
- [ ] **tasty** 形 おいしい
- [ ] **teacher** 名 先生, 教師
- [ ] **tear** 名 涙
- [ ] **tell** 動 ①話す, 言う, 語る ②教える, 知らせる, 伝える ③わかる, 見分ける **tell a lie** うそをつく **tell ～ to …** ～に ～するように言う
- [ ] **than** 接 ～よりも, ～以上に **than usual** いつもより
- [ ] **thank** 動 感謝する, 礼を言う
- [ ] **thankful** 形 ありがたく思う
- [ ] **that** 形 その, あの 代 ①それ, あれ, その［あの］人［物］②《関係代名詞》～である… 接 ～ということ, ～なので, ～だから **so that** ～するために, それで, ～できるように **so ～ that …** 非常に～なので… **such ～ that …** 非常に～なので… 副 そんなに, それほど

The Best of Grimm's Fairy Tales

- **the** 冠 ①その、あの ②《形容詞の前で》～な人々 副《－ ＋比較級、－ ＋比較級》～すればするほど…
- **their** 代 彼(女)らの、それらの
- **them** 代 彼(女)らを[に]、それらを[に]
- **then** 副 その時(に・は)、それから、次に by then その時までに even then その時でさえ from then on それ以来 just then そのとたんに 名 その時 形 その当時の
- **there** 副 ①そこに[で・の]、そこへ、あそこへ ②《－ is [are] ～》～がある[いる] here and there あちこちで over there あそこに there lived ～. ～が住んでいました。 名 そこ
- **these** 代 これら、これ 形 これらの、この
- **they** 代 ①彼(女)らは[が]、それらは[が] ②(一般の)人々は[が]
- **thin** 形 薄い、細い、やせた、まばらな
- **thing** 名 ①物、事 ②《-s》事情、事柄
- **think** 動 思う、考える think of ～のことを考える、～を思いつく、考え出す
- **third** 名 第3(の人[物]) 形 第3の、3番の
- **this** 形 ①この、こちらの、これを ②今の、現在の this minute 今すぐ this one これ、こちら 代 ①これ、この人[物] ②今、ここ at this これを見て、そこで(すぐに) like this このような、こんなふうに
- **thorn** 名 とげ、とげのある植物、いばら
- **thorny** 形 いばらの、とげの多い
- **though** 接 ①～にもかかわらず、～だが ②たとえ～でも as though あたかも～のように、まるで～みたいに even though ～であるけれども、～にもかかわらず 副 しかし
- **thought** 動 think (思う)の過去、過去分詞

- **thread** 名 糸、糸のように細いもの spin into thread 糸につむぐ
- **three** 名 3(の数字)、3人[個] 形 3の、3人[個]の
- **threw** 動 throw (投げる)の過去
- **throne** 名 王座、王権
- **through** 前 ～を通して、～中を[に]、～中 副 ①通して ②終わりまで、まったく、すっかり
- **throughout** 前 ①～中、～を通じて ②～のいたるところに 副 初めから終わりまで、ずっと
- **throw** 動 投げる、浴びせる、ひっかける throw ～ over ～を羽織る
- **thrown** 動 throw (投げる)の過去分詞
- **tie** 動 結ぶ、束縛する tie up ひもで縛る、縛り上げる、つなぐ、拘束する、提携させる
- **till** 前 ～まで(ずっと) 接 ～(する)まで
- **time** 名 ①時、時間、歳月 ②時期 ③期間 ④時代 ⑤回、倍 each time ～するたびに every time ～するときはいつも for some time しばらくの間 for the first time 初めて for the first time in one's life 生まれて初めて in time 間に合って、やがて once upon a time むかしむかし some time いつか、そのうち
- **tire** 動 疲れる、疲れさせる、あきる、あきさせる tire oneself out 疲れきる
- **tired** 動 tire (疲れる)の過去、過去分詞 形 ①疲れた、くたびれた ②あきた、うんざりした get tired of ～に飽きる、～が嫌になる
- **to** 前 ①《方向・変化》～へ、～に、～の方へ ②《程度・時間》～まで ③《適合・付加・所属》～に ④《－ ＋動詞の原形》～するために[の]、～する、～すること
- **today** 名 今日 副 今日(では)
- **together** 副 ①一緒に、ともに ②同時に

Word List

- **told** 動 tell（話す）の過去, 過去分詞
- **tomorrow** 名 明日 副 明日は
- **tonight** 名 今夜, 今晩 副 今夜は
- **too** 副 ①～も（また）②あまりに～すぎる, とても～ far too あまりにも～過ぎる too much 過度の too ～ to …… …するには～すぎる
- **took** 動 take（取る）の過去
- **top** 名 頂上, 首位
- **tore** 動 tear（裂く）の過去
- **touch** 動 ①触れる, さわる, ～を触れさせる ②接触する ③感動させる
- **towards** 前 ①《運動の方向・位置》～の方へ, ～に向かって ②《目的》～のために
- **town** 名 町, 都会, 都市
- **travel** 動 ①旅行する ②進む, 移動する[させる], 伝わる travel on 旅を続ける
- **traveling companion** 旅の連れ
- **tree** 名 木, 樹木
- **trouble** 名 ①困難, 迷惑 ②心配, 苦労 ③もめごと it is too much trouble to ～するのはあまりに面倒である
- **troubled** 形《be –》憂慮する
- **true** 形 ①本当の, 本物の, 真の ②誠実な, 確かな come true 実現する
- **trunk** 名 ①幹, 胴 ②本体, 主要部分 ③トランク, 旅行かばん
- **truth** 名 ①真理, 事実, 本当 ②誠実, 忠実さ
- **try** 動 ①やってみる, 試みる ②努力する, 努める
- **turn** 動 ①ひっくり返す, 回転する[させる], 曲がる, 曲げる, 向かう, 向ける ②(～に)なる, (～に)変える turn into ～に変わる turn to ～の方を向く 名 ①回転, 曲がり ②順番 ③変化, 転換 do ～ a good turn ～を助ける
- **twelve** 名 12（の数字）, 12人[個] 形 12の, 12人[個]の
- **twice** 副 2倍, 2度, 2回
- **two** 名 2（の数字）, 2人[個] 形 2の, 2人[個]の
- **tying** 動 tie（結ぶ）の現在分詞

U

- **unable** 形《be – to ～》～することができない
- **under** 前 ①《位置》～の下に[で] ②《状態》～で, ～を受けて, ～のもと ③《数量》～以下[未満]の, ～より下の
- **underground** 形 地下の[にある]
- **understand** 動 理解する, わかる, ～を聞いて知っている
- **uneasy** 形 不安な, 焦って
- **unhappily** 副 不幸に, 運悪く, 不愉快そうに
- **unhappy** 形 不運な, 不幸な
- **unhurt** 形 傷ついていない, 無傷の
- **unicorn** 名 一角獣, ユニコーン
- **unkindly** 形 不親切な, 意地悪な
- **unpack** 動 (包み・荷を)解いて中身を出す
- **unpleasant** 形 不愉快な, 気にさわる, いやな, 不快な
- **until** 前 ～まで(ずっと) 接 ～の時まで, ～するまで
- **up** 副 ①上へ, 上がって, 北へ ②立って, 近づいて ③向上して, 増して up and down 上がったり下がったり, 行ったり来たり, あちこち up to ～まで, ～に至るまで, ～に匹敵して 前 ①～の上(の方)へ, 高い方へ ②(道)に沿って
- **upon** 前 ①《場所・接触》～(の上)に ②《日・時》～に ③《関係・従事》～に関して, ～について, ～して
- **upset** 形 憤慨して, 動揺して 動 気を悪くさせる, (心・神経など)をかき乱す
- **upstairs** 副 2階へ[に], 階上へ

141

- **us** 代 私たちを[に]
- **use** 動 ①使う, 用いる ②費やす 名 使用, 用途 **no use** 役に立たない, 用をなさない
- **used** 動 ①use(使う)の過去, 過去分詞 ②《- to》よく～したものだ, 以前は～であった 形 ①慣れている, 《get [become] - to》～に慣れてくる ②使われた, 中古の
- **useful** 形 役に立つ, 有効な, 有益な
- **usual** 形 通常の, いつもの, 平常の, 普通の **as usual** いつものように, 相変わらず **than usual** いつもより

V

- **very** 副 とても, 非常に, まったく 形 本当の, きわめて, まさしくその
- **voice** 名 声, 音声

W

- **wait** 動 ①待つ, 《- for ～》～を待つ ②延ばす, 延ばせる, 遅らせる ③《- on [upon] ～》～に仕える, 給仕をする
- **wake** 動 ①目がさめる, 起きる, 起こす ②奮起する **wake up** 起きる, 目を覚ます **wake up to** ～に気付く, ～で目を覚ます
- **walk** 動 歩く, 歩かせる, 散歩する **walk along** (前へ)歩く, ～に沿って歩く **walk around** 歩き回る, ぶらぶら歩く **walk away** 立ち去る, 遠ざかる **walk on** 歩き続ける **walk to** ～まで歩いて行く
- **wall** 名 壁, 塀 **against the wall** 壁を背にして
- **wand** 名 杖
- **want** 動 ほしい, 望む, ～したい, ～してほしい
- **war** 名 戦争(状態), 闘争, 不和
- **was** 動 《beの第1・第3人称単数現在 am, isの過去》～であった, (～に)いた[あった]
- **wash** 動 ①洗う, 洗濯する ②押し流す[される] **wash away** 押し流す
- **watch** 動 ①じっと見る, 見物する ②注意[用心]する, 監視する **watch over** 見守る, 見張る
- **water** 名 ①水 ②(川・湖・海などの)多量の水
- **waterhole** 名 水たまり, 泉
- **wave** 名 波 動 (手などを振って)合図する
- **way** 名 ①道, 通り道 ②方向, 距離 ③方法, 手段 ④習慣 **a little way** 少し **all the way** ずっと, はるばる, いろいろと **find one's way** たどり着く **in any way** 決して, 多少なりとも **long way** はるかに **on one's way** 途中で **on the way** 途中で **way out** 出口, 逃げ道, 脱出方法, 解決法 **way out of** ～から抜け出る道 **way to** ～する方法 **go on one's way** 道を進む, 立ち去る
- **we** 代 私たちは[が]
- **weak** 形 ①弱い, 力のない, 病弱な ②劣った, へたな, 苦手な
- **weather** 名 天気, 天候, 空模様
- **wedding** 名 結婚式, 婚礼
- **week** 名 週, 1週間
- **weight** 名 ①重さ, 重力, 体重 ②重荷, 負担 ③重大さ, 勢力
- **welcome** 動 歓迎する 形 歓迎される, 自由に～してよい **most welcome** 大歓迎
- **well** 副 ①うまく, 上手に ②十分に, よく, かなり **as well** なお, その上, 同様に **as well as** ～と同様に 間 へえ, まあ, ええと 名 井戸
- **well-known** 形 よく知られた, 有名な
- **went** 動 go(行く)の過去
- **were** 動 《beの2人称単数・複数の過去》～であった, (～に)いた[あった]
- **wet** 形 ぬれた, 湿った, 雨の **wet**

WORD LIST

- **through** びしょぬれになって 動 ぬらす, ぬれる
- **what** 代 ①何が[を・に] ②《関係代名詞》～するところのもの[こと] 形 ①何の, どんな ②なんと ③～するだけの 副 いかに, どれほど **what sort of** どういう **What (～) for?** 何のために, なぜ **what … for** どんな目的で **What's up?** 何があったのですか。やあ, どうですか。
- **wheel** 名 輪, 車輪
- **when** 副 ①いつ ②《関係副詞》～するところの, ～するとその時, ～するとき 接 ～の時, ～するとき 代 いつ
- **where** 副 ①どこに[で] ②《関係副詞》～するところの, そしてそこで, ～するところに[へ], ～するところに[へ] 代 ①どこ, どの点 ②～するところの
- **whether** 接 ～かどうか, ～かまたは…, ～であろうとなかろうと
- **which** 形 ①どちらの, どの, どれでも ②どんな～でも, そしてこの 代 ①どちら, どれ, どの人[物] ②《関係代名詞》～するところの **of which** ～の中で
- **while** 接 ①～の間(に), ～する間(に) ②一方, ～なのに 名 しばらくの間, 一定の時 **after a while** しばらくして **for a while** しばらくの間, 少しの間
- **white** 形 ①白い, (顔色などが)青ざめた ②白人の 名 白, 白色
- **who** 代 ①誰が[は], どの人 ②《関係代名詞》～するところの(人)
- **whoever** 代 ～する人は誰でも, 誰が～しようとも
- **whole** 形 全体の, すべての, 完全な, 満～, 丸～
- **why** 副 ①なぜ, どうして ②《関係副詞》～するところの(理由) 間 ①おや, まあ ②もちろん, なんだって ③ええと
- **wife** 名 妻, 夫人
- **wild** 形 ①野生の ②荒涼として ③荒っぽい ④奇抜な
- **will** 動 ～だろう, ～しよう, する(つもりだ) **will have done** ～してしまっているだろう《未来進行形》**Will you ～?** ～してくれませんか。
- **win** 動 勝つ, 獲得する, 達する
- **wind** 名 ①風 ②うねり, 一巻き
- **winding road** 曲がりくねった道, ワインディング・ロード
- **window** 名 窓, 窓ガラス
- **wine** 名 ワイン, ぶどう酒
- **wish** 動 望む, 願う, (～であればよいと)思う **wish for** 所望する **wish someone good day** (人)の一日の幸運を祈る 名 (心からの)願い
- **witch** 名 魔法使い, 魔女
- **with** 前 ①《同伴・付随・所属》～と一緒に, ～を身につけて, ～とともに ②《様態》～(の状態)で, ～して ③《手段・道具》～で, ～を使って **do with** ～を処理する **go with** ～と一緒に行く, ～と調和する, ～にとても似合う
- **within** 前 ①～の中[内]に, ～の内部に ②～以内で, ～を越えないで
- **without** 前 ～なしで, ～がなく, ～しないで
- **woke** 動 wake (目が覚める)の過去
- **woman** 名 (成人した)女性, 婦人
- **women** 名 woman (女性)の複数
- **won't** will notの短縮形
- **wonder** 動 ①不思議に思う, (～に)驚く ②(～かしらと)思う
- **wonderful** 形 驚くべき, すばらしい, すてきな
- **wood** 名 ①《しばしば-s》森, 林 ②木材, まき **out of the wood** 森の中から出て
- **woodcutter** 名 木こり
- **woodcutting** 名 木材伐採
- **word** 名 ①語, 単語 ②ひと言 ③《one's -》約束
- **work** 動 ①働く, 勉強する, 取り組

む ②機能[作用]する, うまくいく 名①仕事, 勉強 ②職 ③作品
- **workman** 名労働者, 職人
- **workmen** 名 workman (労働者) の複数
- **world** 名《the -》世界, ～界 in the world 世界で
- **worry** 動悩む, 悩ませる, 心配する[させる]
- **worth** 形 (～の) 価値がある, (～) しがいがある
- **would** 助《will の過去》①～するだろう, ～するつもりだ ②～したものだ would like to ～したいと思う would rather ～する方がよい
- **written** 動 write (書く) の過去分詞
- **wrong** 形①間違った, (道徳上)悪い ②調子が悪い, 故障した go wrong 失敗する, 道を踏みはずす, 調子が悪くなる 副間違って
- **wrote** 動 write (書く) の過去

Y

- **yard** 名庭
- **year** 名①年, 1年 ②学年, 年度 ③ ～歳 for years 何年も for ～ years ～年間, ～年にわたって
- **yell** 動大声をあげる, わめく
- **yelling** 名どなり声
- **yes** 副はい, そうです
- **yesterday** 名①昨日 ②過ぎし日, 昨今 副昨日 (は)
- **you** 代①あなた (方) は[が], あなた (方) を[に] ②(一般に) 人は
- **young** 形若い, 幼い, 青年の
- **your** 代あなた (方) の
- **yourself** 代あなた自身
- **yourselves** 代 yourself (あなた自身) の複数

E-CAT

English **C**onversational **A**bility **T**est
国際英語会話能力検定

● E-CATとは…
英語が話せるようになるためのテストです。インターネットベースで、30分であなたの発話力をチェックします。

www.ecatexam.com

iTEP

● iTEP®とは…
世界各国の企業、政府機関、アメリカの大学300校以上が、英語能力判定テストとして採用。オンラインによる90分のテストで文法、リーディング、リスニング、ライティング、スピーキングの5技能をスコア化。iTEP®は、留学、就職、海外赴任などに必要な、世界に通用する英語力を総合的に評価する画期的なテストです。

www.itepexamjapan.com

ラダーシリーズ

The Best of Grimm's Fairy Tales グリム名作選

2012年4月5日　第1刷発行
2025年3月3日　第13刷発行

原著者　グリム兄弟

発行者　賀川　洋

発行所　IBCパブリッシング株式会社
〒162-0804 東京都新宿区中里町29番3号
菱秀神楽坂ビル
Tel. 03-3513-4511　Fax. 03-3513-4512
www.ibcpub.co.jp

© IBC Publishing, Inc. 2012

印刷　株式会社シナノパブリッシングプレス

装丁　伊藤 理恵　　本文イラスト　目黒 久美子

組版データ　ITC Berkeley Oldstyle Pro Medium+Britannic Bold Regular

落丁本・乱丁本は、小社宛にお送りください。送料小社負担にてお取り替えいたします。
本書の無断複写（コピー）は著作権法上での例外を除き禁じられています。

Printed in Japan
ISBN 978-4-7946-0136-0

カバーイラスト：『ヘンゼルとグレーテル』 (Arthur Rackham, 1909, Wikipedia)

※本書はラダーシリーズ『グリム傑作童話集 (Grimms' Fairy Tales)』と
『グリム・クラシックス (Grimms' Classics)』を元に再構成したものです。